THE PARADOX OF REPRESENTATION

THE PARADOX
OF REPRESENTATION

RACIAL GERRYMANDERING AND
MINORITY INTERESTS IN CONGRESS

David Lublin

PRINCETON UNIVERSITY PRESS

PRINCETON, NEW JERSEY

SECOND PRINTING, AND FIRST PAPERBACK PRINTING, 1999

PAPERBACK ISBN 0-691-01010-2

THE LIBRARY OF CONGRESS HAS CATALOGED THE CLOTH EDITION

OF THIS BOOK AS FOLLOWS

LUBLIN, DAVID, 1968–

THE PARADOX OF REPRESENTATION : RACIAL GERRYMANDERING

AND MINORITY INTERESTS IN CONGRESS / DAVID LUBLIN.

P. CM.

INCLUDES BIBLIOGRAPHICAL REFERENCES (P.) AND INDEX.

ISBN 0-691-02669-6 (ALK. PAPER)

1. GERRYMANDERING—UNITED STATES.

2. UNITED STATES. CONGRESS. HOUSE—ELECTION DISTRICTS.

3. ELECTION DISTRICTS—UNITED STATES.   4. AFRO-AMERICAN LEGISLATORS

5. HISPANIC AMERICAN LEGISLATORS.   I. TITLE.

JK1341.L83   1997   328.73′073455—dc21   96-45560

THIS BOOK HAS BEEN COMPOSED IN BITSTREAM CALEDONIA

THE PAPER USED IN THIS PUBLICATION MEETS THE

MINIMUM REQUIREMENTS OF ANSI/NISO Z39.48-1992

(R1997) (*PERMANENCE OF PAPER*)

http://pup.princeton.edu

PRINTED IN THE UNITED STATES OF AMERICA

3   5   7   9   10   8   6   4   2

TO MY PARENTS

Janet and Edward Lublin

CONTENTS

LIST OF FIGURES AND TABLES

Figures

Tables

PREFACE

THE VOTING RIGHTS ACT of 1965 marked a key victory of the civil rights movement. Thanks to this ground-breaking legislation, African Americans no longer face mortal danger in exercising their right to vote. African-American and Latino struggles to gain representation have shifted from ballot access to redistricting since 1965. The Voting Rights Act, as amended in 1982, effectively forced states to maximize the number of majority-minority districts during the 1990 redistricting round.

Supporters as well as opponents of racial redistricting invoke the language and goals of the civil rights movement in order to legitimate their position. Opponents denounce racial redistricting as fundamentally inimical to the goal of a racially blind society. Racial redistricting, they argue, amounts to political segregation that can only further fragment and racialize American politics. Civil rights advocates counter that majority-minority districts remain vital to the election of minority candidates and the inclusion of minorities in the policy-making process. Neither the courts nor the politicians have resolved this question: does racial redistricting advance minority representation?

The Paradox of Representation analyzes the link between race and representation to answer this question. Packing blacks into 65 percent black or greater districts is no longer necessary at the congressional level in most parts of the country since African Americans regularly carry all majority black districts. Majority-minority districts nevertheless are crucial to election of significant numbers of African-American and Latino representatives. African Americans and Latinos almost never win election from white majority districts.

African-American representatives are more than symbols or role models. They are clearly more responsive to black policy preferences than any other group of representatives. Ironically, racial redistricting makes the House as a whole less likely to adopt policies favored by blacks. Concentrating black voters in a few districts increases their influence over a small group of black representatives but reduces their influence over the entire House. Judicial efforts to curb creative gerrymanders that protect Democrats while drawing additional black districts will make the trade-off more acute. Following recent court decisions, redistricters must now either draw majority-minority districts more compactly or eliminate them.

African Americans face a painful dilemma that leaves blacks with two rather unpalatable choices: an unresponsive Congress or few black representatives. Compromise and balance are badly needed. Most discussions present racial redistricting as an all-or-nothing choice betweeen two competing visions and value systems. This approach severely constrains policy options. Maximizing the number of black majority districts undercuts black influence even as the number of African-American representatives increases. At the same time, expecting high numbers of blacks to win election without racial redistricting seems overly optimistic. Between 1788 and 1994, only six African Americans won election from districts with white majorities. Jointly maximizing black descriptive and substantive representation will most likely require withdrawing partially from the maximization strategy pursued during the 1990 redistricting round.

Controversies over race hinge on terminology, so a short note on terms is appropriate. *African American* and *black* are used throughout as synonyms. *Latino* and *Hispanic* are also used as synonyms. *White* usually refers only to non-Hispanic whites but refers to all nonblacks or non-Latinos in some cases that should be clear from the context. *Percent black* and *percent Latino* refer to the percentage of blacks and Latinos in the total population unless I specifically note that the percentage is of the voting-age population instead.

So many people contributed to the completion of this book. Gary King constantly spurred me to improve this work and to relentlessly pursue the answers to my questions. Katherine Tate provided strong support even as she constantly forced me to rethink my conclusions. Gary and Katherine both took the time for thoroughly enjoyable spirited arguments about race and redistricting that greatly improved the analysis. Paul Peterson encouraged me to write on this topic and gave me several opportunities to present my early findings. Tami Buhr, the best of friends and colleagues, provided sound advice and much-needed support from this work's inception through its completion. Steve Voss shared his insightful comments on more occasions than I can remember. Sue Ikenberry regularly injected perspective and common sense. Maryjane Osa helped tighten the final text and made me laugh. David Canon, James Garand, Bernard Grofman, Marc Lipsitch, and Richard Pildes all read preliminary versions of this manuscript and provided helpful comments. The participants of the Workshops on Race, Ethnicity, Governance and Participation at Harvard University shared a variety of thoughtful comments. Patricia Freedman and Patrick Eugene located numerous legal cases for me on very short notice. The sharp political controversy over racial redistricting makes the author's traditional taking of all responsibility for the conclusions and mistakes contained in this volume particularly appropriate here.

Greatest thanks of all must go to my family. Everyone deserves at least one person in their life who thinks that they are just terrific come hell or high water. I've had two. Gladys Mehler and Rosalyn Weiss, my grandmothers, served as my greatest cheerleaders ever since I can remember. My sister, Jennifer, applauded louder than anyone as I made progress. Most of all, I owe an enormous debt of love and thanks to my parents, Janet and Edward Lublin. My parents shaped my views on race from an early age and then completely supported me when I chose to study, and ultimately write about, race and politics. If there is any content to my character, it is due to them.

THE PARADOX OF REPRESENTATION

1

INTRODUCTION

Central Issues and Approach

THE CREATION of new majority-minority districts to advance minority representation has been one of the most controversial aspects of the Voting Rights Act since its inception in 1965. Advocates of racial redistricting deem it essential to the election of African-American and Latino representatives and the expression of minority political opinions in the halls of power. Opponents decry this policy as going beyond the original scope of the act and perpetuating racial distinctions in both law and society. They further contend that African Americans and Latinos can win elections without the aid of racial gerrymanders and that drawing new majority-minority districts actually harms minority efforts to advance their policy goals by reducing minority electoral influence over all but a small subset of representatives.

Recent events have heightened the controversy over promoting minority representation through racial redistricting. Many states created new majority-minority districts with highly irregular boundaries during the 1990 redistricting round. The Supreme Court placed the entire racial redistricting strategy under a legal cloud by ruling in *Miller v. Johnson* that using race as the "predominant factor" in drawing district lines violates the Equal Protection Clause. This book provides a gauge of progress made under the Voting Rights Act by using statistical analysis to measure the empirical effect of racial redistricting on both the election of minority officials and public policy. This study should thus allow for assessment of the efficacy of advancing minority representation through racial redistricting.

In this work, I demonstrate the following:

1. Racial redistricting in the South has made the House less likely to adopt legislation favored by African Americans. Racial redistricting in the North generally does not have the same effect.

2. Racial redistricting results in the election of more Republicans unless mapmakers purposively adopt Democratic gerrymanders with bizarre district lines to avoid this outcome. The creation of new majority-minority districts assured that the Republicans won solid control of the House in 1994.

3. Black influence districts most strongly increase the responsiveness of representatives to black concerns if African Americans compose at least 40 percent of the population. African Americans usually cannot elect black represen-

tatives in 40 to 50 percent black districts without the aid of coalition partners, particularly Latinos, but their votes effectively veto the election of conservative representatives.

4. Except for districts represented by northern Democrats, increasing the African-American population above or below the 40 percent black threshold raises the responsiveness of representatives in both white and black majority districts. Regional differences in the the dispersion of blacks and ideology of whites explain this variation in responsiveness across regions. Southern Democrats pay close attention to the racial balance in their districts because of the relative conservatism of most southern whites compared to most southern blacks. The lack of responsiveness to changes in the black share of the population by northern representatives reflects that nonblack liberals live in close proximity to black districts in the North. Representatives of these districts can maintain liberal policy stances regardless of the black share of the population because of high levels of white support for liberalism.

5. The election of more than token numbers of African-American and Latino representatives requires drawing majority-minority districts. The substantial increase in the election of African-American and Latino representatives over the past thirty years rests entirely on the creation of new black districts.

6. The so-called 65 percent rule is invalid. Some advocates of minority representation have argued that minorities must comprise at least 65 percent of the population in a district in order to assure the election of a black or Latino official. Empirical analysis indicates that 55 percent minority districts should elect minority representatives to the House in most portions of the country.

7. Increasing the percentage of Latinos in a district reduces the percentage of blacks required to promote the election of a black representative.

8. The percentage of Latinos in a district needed to assure the election of a Latino representative rises as the percentage of citizens declines.

Overview of the Voting Rights Act

Outlining the major provisions of the Voting Rights Act of 1965 helps illuminate the debate over the breadth of its application. Reiterating the guarantees of the Fifteenth Amendment, Section 2 prohibits the adoption of voting qualifications that restrict or deny the right to the vote on the basis of race. Section 4 of the act suspended the use of any "tests and devices" to qualify voters for five years in "covered" jurisdictions. This section defined as "covered" any jurisdiction that had a test for registering or voting as of November 1, 1964 and in which under 50 percent of the voting-age population voted or was registered to vote in the 1964 presidential election. This carefully targeted provision originally captured six southern states (Alabama, Georgia,

Louisiana, Mississippi, South Carolina, and Virginia) and portions of a seventh (North Carolina).

Section 5 mandates that covered jurisdictions preclear any changes in "any voting qualification or prerequisite to voting, or standard, practice, or procedure with respect to voting different from that in force on November 1, 1964" with either the U.S. District Court for the District of Columbia or the U.S. attorney general. Sections 6 and 7 require the Civil Service Commission to send federal registrars to covered jurisdictions upon certification by the attorney general of either the receipt of twenty meritorious complaints "alleging that they have been denied the right to vote under color of law on account of race or color" or that the appointment of examiners is vital for enforcement of the Fifteenth Amendment. Section 3 allows the courts to apply Sections 4 through 7 to any jurisdiction, covered or not, if the court deems the suspension of tests for voting or the appointment of federal registrars necessary to enforce the Fifteenth Amendment. Section 8 of the act provides for the appointment of poll watchers to monitor the election process in jurisdictions covered under either Sections 3 or 4 of the act.

Provisions in the original version of the act allowed covered jurisdictions to bail out from coverage if they could prove to the U.S. District Court for the District of Columbia that they had not used a discriminatory test for voting for at least five years. Extensions of the act have repeatedly lengthened the time without a discriminatory test needed to bail out under these provisions. These changes have effectively prevented any jurisdiction from bailing out from coverage under Sections 4 through 8 of the act.[1] Congress extended the act in 1970, 1975, and 1982, and amendments broadened the act's application to new areas of the country and language minorities.

Racial Redistricting and the Voting Rights Act

The provisions of the Voting Rights Act collectively proved potent tools in the fight to extend the franchise to African Americans. African-American participation in the political process rose considerably, and the racial gap in registration and voting substantially declined after the passage of the act.[2] The entry of black voters into the political arena was merely the first step toward advancing black representation. Voting rights advocates recognized that the inability of blacks to elect African-American officials from white majority districts greatly limited the impact of the act on black representation. The single-member-plurality district system used for electing members of the House usually results in minorities receiving a much smaller share of seats than they would under a system of proportional representation. Minority votes do not effectively translate into a proportionate share of seats unless geographical concentration allows minorities to dominate in various regions. Some nations, including France and Italy, have adopted single-member district electoral systems precisely to reduce divisiveness within the legislature by eliminating minority parties.

The drawing of new majority-minority districts has been central to the strategy for advancing minority representation. Advocates of greater minority representation hope to overcome the barriers present in the winner-take-all aspect of the single-member-plurality district system to minority representation by consciously creating majority-minority districts. Proponents of majority-minority districts have vigorously argued for a broad interpretation of Sections 2 and 5 in the hopes of forcing the creation of new majority-minority districts. Laws that dilute the impact of minority votes, as well as laws that disenfranchise minorities, are subject to preclearance under Section 5 under the broad interpretation. This interpretation allows the attorney general to force states to draw new majority-minority districts in order to obtain preclearance for redistricting plans. Minorities can file suit to enjoin states to create new majority-minority districts if the attorney general fails to vigorously promote the drawing of new majority-minority constituencies. Opponents of the broad interpretation read the Voting Rights Act narrowly to apply strictly to laws governing access to the ballot.

The proponents of the broad interpretation had until recently gradually won greater acceptance for their position in the Congress and the courts. The Voting Rights Act did not strictly require the creation of new black districts, but court decisions combined with the provisions of the act forced states to draw new majority-minority districts or face opposition to their redistricting plans from the Justice Department and the courts. Congress intervened to overturn the Court's ruling when the Supreme Court temporarily veered away from its support for an interpretation of the act favoring the creation of new black districts.

The creation of new majority-minority districts in the aftermath of the 1990 reapportionment caused the greatest upheaval in congressional district boundaries since the Supreme Court forced states to minimize population deviations between districts in the mid-1960s. The 1982 amendments to the Voting Rights Act set this process in motion. These amendments effectively institutionalized the broad interpretation of the act by requiring the Department of Justice and the judiciary to examine the effect of electoral laws, including redistricting plans, on minority vote dilution. The amendments and the Supreme Court decision upholding their constitutionality followed the 1980 reapportionment, so the major push for new majority-minority districts did not begin until the 1990s. Many states drew sprawling districts with con-

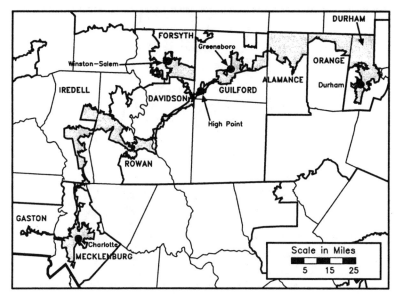

1.1. Twelfth District of North Carolina, 1992.
Source: Map © Election Data Services, Inc.

voluted lines that utterly disregarded county and city boundaries as part of their effort to concentrate blacks and Latinos into new majority-minority districts during the 1990 redistricting cycle. States created fifteen new black majority districts and ten new Latino majority districts between 1990 and 1992. This increase in the number of majority-minority districts reignited a major debate over the efficacy of racial redistricting in advancing minority representation as well as the legality and the morality of consciously drawing congressional districts along racial lines.

North Carolina's new Twelfth District, pictured in figure 1.1, is arguably the most extreme example of racial redistricting. This district links a narrow ribbon of black population concentrations in Gastonia, Charlotte, Winston-Salem, Greensboro, and Durham along Interstate 85. The I-85 district can be considered contiguous under only the most charitable of definitions. The district occasionally narrows to the width of one lane of I-85 and is at times contiguous only at points. The Twelfth District may epitomize racial gerrymandering, but it is hardly unique. Florida has several bizarrely shaped districts. The Third District in the northern part of the state resembles a necklace in the way it strings together black communities in that portion of the state (see fig. 1.2). Florida created several snakelike districts in the Miami area as part of its effort to separate whites, blacks, and Latinos into separate districts.

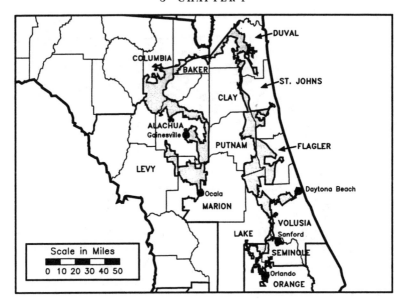

1.2. Third District of Florida, 1992.
Source: Map © Election Data Services, Inc.

Reaction and Criticism of Racial Redistricting

This long-term effort to promote new majority-minority districts paid massive dividends in the form of numerous new majority-minority districts following the 1990 reapportionment. The strategy of promoting new majority-minority districts brought the Voting Rights Act under increased legal and public scrutiny. Many opponents of racial redistricting question the legality and constitutionality of this policy. Conservatives have further attacked racial redistricting as unnecessary to promote minority representation. Liberals contend that the racial redistricting has not effectively gained real political influence for minorities. Some observers attack racial redistricting as unethical because it requires that the government treat citizens differently on the basis of race.

The Legality of Racial Redistricting

Just after civil rights advocates achieved substantial gains in the number of minority elected officials in the 1992 elections, the Supreme Court cast doubt on the entire legal basis for these gains. The Supreme Court stated in its opinion in *Shaw v. Reno* that racial gerrymanders are justiciable under the Equal Protection Clause of the Constitution. The Court dealt a serious blow to efforts to maintain the new majority-minority districts by ruling in *Miller v. Johnson* that using race as the "predominant factor" in drawing district lines violates the Equal Protection Clause. Litigation stemming from this decision may erase the large gains made by blacks and Latinos in the 1992 elections.

Some supporters of a narrow interpretation of the act also contend that the original version of the act was not intended to allow federal review of laws that did not directly limit minority access to the franchise. Abigail Thernstrom, the leading proponent of this position, forcefully argues that sponsors of the Voting Rights Act conceived of it as a limited, short-term unusual exertion of federal power designed to eliminate a particularly intractable form of discrimination. African Americans gained the means to defend their own interests without the aid of special racially based federal protection once they won access to the ballot. The expansion of the act constitutes unwarranted and unnecessary intrusion by the federal government into the power of states to make laws, according to Thernstrom.

Opponents of this view convincingly argue that legislative history shows that the Voting Rights Act was not conceived with such a narrow purpose. Writing for a majority of the Supreme Court in *Allen v. State Board of Elections*, Chief Justice Earl Warren expressed strong agreement with the broad interpretation of the act as early as 1969. The chief justice stated:

> We must reject the narrow construction that appellees would give to Section 5. The Voting Rights Act was aimed at the subtle, as well as the obvious, state regulations that have the effect of denying citizens their right to vote because of their race. Moreover, compatible with the decisions of the Court, the Act gives a broad interpretation to the right to vote, recognizing that voting includes "all action necessary to make a vote effective. . . ." The right to vote can be affected by a dilution of voting power as well as by an absolute prohibition on casting a ballot.[3]

The Court has occasionally tried to limit the breadth of the application of the act despite Chief Justice Warren's forceful argument for a broad interpretation. *Miller v. Johnson* marks a clear shift toward the more conservative interpretation of the act. The Court nevertheless failed to endorse the strict narrow construction of the act embraced by Thernstrom even in *Miller*. The "predominant factor" standard outlined by the Court in *Miller* cuts both ways. It bars states from adopting plans intended to dilute minority votes by reducing the number of majority-minority districts just as it prohibits racial gerrymanders designed to advantage minorities.[4]

The Efficacy of Racial Redistricting

The most potent argument against racial redistricting may be that it fails to achieve the goal of advancing black representation. Abigail Thernstrom and Carol Swain argue that minorities can win election from majority white districts. Critics of racial redistricting contend that concentrating minorities into a few districts limits minority influence over public policy. Creating new majority-minority districts requires shifting minorities out of adjoining majority white districts. Minorities gain control over the representative from the majority-minority district at the cost of losing influence over several representatives in majority white districts. Racial redistricting may result in greater racial polarization in the legislature. The election of more conservative white representatives from newly overwhelmingly white districts may accompany the election of greater numbers of liberal African American and Latino representatives from new majority-minority districts.

Democrats fear and Republicans hope that racial redistricting will produce exactly this result. Republicans think that packing liberal Democratic minority voters into a few districts made adjoining districts more conservative and Republican and helped them win control of the House in 1994. This result would be deliciously ironic for Republicans. White Democrats would have been the major losers from a political version of exactly the type of affirmative action policy generally supported by Democrats and opposed by Republicans. The election of greater numbers of minority representatives may prove a pyrrhic victory for the African-American and Latino communities if racial redistricting did swell the size of the House Republican Caucus. Opposition to the liberal policies favored by most black and Latino legislators stiffened within the House just as their numbers increased. Racial redistricting may increase the number of minority representatives but leave them relatively powerless in a Congress dominated by conservatives.

Some members of the civil rights community have joined the conservatives in questioning the efficacy of majority-minority districts in advancing minority representation. Lani Guinier, President Clinton's controversial nominee for the post of assistant attorney general for civil rights, labels the majority-minority districting strategy "the triumph of tokenism" and suggests that gains in the election of new minority representatives mask a failure to achieve true equality of opportunity in the political arena. African-American and Latino representatives may not truly have a fair share in the decision-making process in a legislative arena based on majority rule. Guinier's arguments suggest the adoption of electoral and governing rules like those used during the transition from white rule in South Africa. Proportional representation prevented the exclusion of minorities in parliament. Minorities also gained access to power because the interim constitution required the inclusion of all parties of a certain size in the government.[5]

Both the conservative and liberal critiques of the efficacy of new majority-minority districts in advancing minority representation suggest that the debate over racial redistricting would greatly benefit from an analysis of the impact of the Voting Rights Act on minority representation. The moral and legal debates fade in importance if majority-minority districts prove unnecessary to assure the election of blacks and Latinos to Congress or if they fail to enhance the influence of minority representatives over public policy. A quantitative analysis of the relationship between aggregate district characteristics, including the racial composition of districts, and the race of a district's representative will shed light on the necessity of majority-minority districts for the election of more than token numbers of blacks and Latinos to Congress. Statistical analysis of aggregate district characteristics and roll-call voting behavior on the floor of the House will make it possible to evaluate the Voting Rights Act's success in promoting pro-black representation and to compare the strategy embodied by racial redistricting with alternative ones. This study will thus bring long-needed nonideologically driven data analysis to bear on what have largely been normative debates about race and representation. This work has a bias in favor of advancing minority representation, but I judge which strategy best achieves that goal through empirical analysis, rather than intuition or anecdotal evidence.

The Morality of Racial Redistricting

The drawing of majority-minority districts has been attacked on moral grounds. The conscious drawing of majority-minority districts troubles some precisely because the Voting Rights Act of 1965 grew out of a movement dedicated to making America a nonracial democracy. Dr. Martin Luther King Jr.'s call to judge people not by "the color of their skin but by the content of their character" resonated so powerfully with all Americans because it grounded the demand for equal justice in America's own values.[6] The contrast between the ideal of equal access to the political process and the reality of white supremacists denying members of racial minorities access to the ballot, the most fundamental instrument of our democracy, solely on the basis of race helped propel the Voting Rights Act through Congress.[7] All race-conscious redistricting is arguably corrosive to efforts to build a nonracial democracy. As Justice Sandra Day O'Connor explained in *Shaw v. Reno*, "Racial gerrymandering, even for remedial purposes, may balkanize us into competing racial factions; it threatens to carry us further from the goal of a political system in which race no longer matters—a goal that the Fourteenth and Fifteenth Amendments embody, and to which the Nation continues to aspire."[8] The Court could not stomach the overtly racial nature of the districting process and declared districting plans motivated predominantly by race unconstitutional in *Miller v. Johnson, Shaw v. Hunt,* and *Bush v. Vera.*

Voting rights debates in the 1990s continually provide a contrast between ideals and realities in spite of the Supreme Court's ruling. African Americans and Latinos would ideally not find it so difficult to gain election from majority non-Hispanic white constituencies. The single-member-plurality district system may seem value neutral on the surface, but it undermines the election of political minorities of any stripe. Racial redistricting may not appeal either morally or aesthetically, but the failure of Alabama, Florida, North Carolina, South Carolina, and Virginia to elect a single African-American member of Congress until the creation of black majority districts for the 1992 elections poses moral problems as well.[9] America can hardly construe itself as the country in which any kid can grow up to become president if its African-American and Latino citizens cannot even win election to Congress. Racial redistricting may be the only way to overcome the discriminatory tendencies of the single-member-plurality district electoral system without completely scraping the system itself.

Definitions: Descriptive and Substantive Representation

Analyzing the impact of the Voting Rights Act on black representation requires defining the meaning of representation. Hanna Pitkin makes a valuable distinction between descriptive and substantive representation.[10] Members of minority groups win descriptive representation in the political arena by electing members of their group to public office. Minority groups gain substantive representation by exerting influence over the policy process. Descriptive representation can serve as a mechanism for gaining substantive representation. Observers often perceive the first elections of black representatives to Congress in a state as a great symbolic advance for the black community. The symbolism exists precisely because African Americans expect these newly elected representatives to more effectively press for substantive policy changes than their white predecessors. Minorities presumably do not achieve long-term satisfaction from increases in descriptive representation if concrete changes in public policy do not follow these symbolic advances.

Minority groups may nevertheless gain substantive representation without descriptive representation. Minorities may possess the power to effectively pressure and persuade their elected officials to respond to their concerns even if they cannot elect one of their members to office. Black voters remain a voting bloc critical to the reelection of many white Democratic representatives, particularly those elected from the South.[11] These representatives ignore the concerns of the black community at their peril.

Overview of the Book

Part I of this book focuses on African-American and Latino descriptive representation. Chapter 2 outlines the historical success of blacks and Latinos in gaining election to the House of Representatives prior to examining the growth of majority-minority districts and minority representation in the post-Voting Rights era. Chapter 3 presents a statistical analysis of factors contributing to the election of African-American and Latino representatives.

Part II turns to an analysis of minority substantive representation. Chapter 4 studies the ideology, partisanship, seniority, and electoral success of African-American, Latino, and white representatives. Chapter 5 presents a statistical analysis of the link between the racial composition of a congressional district and the substantive representation of black interests on the floor of the House of Representatives in order to provide a basis for comparing the substantive representation of minority and nonminority members of Congress. Chapter 6 outlines the implications of the results from chapter 5 for strategies to maximize black representation through redistricting. Unlike earlier chapters, chapters 5 and 6 do not examine Latino as well as African-American representation. Representatives cannot really be expected to respond to changes in the proportion of Latinos in a district in the same way as they do to changes in the proportion of whites and African Americans due to the much lower level of turnout among Latinos. The diversity of opinion within and between Latino national subgroups makes it difficult to determine exactly how members of Congress influenced by Latinos should act. Chapter 7 discusses the results and current legal cases involving racial redistricting and their implications for future action and minority representation.

PART I

BLACK AND LATINO DESCRIPTIVE

REPRESENTATION

2

THE HISTORY OF BLACK AND

LATINO REPRESENTATION

THE GOAL OF this study is to determine if racial redistricting under the aegis of the Voting Rights Act has advanced the descriptive and substantive representation of African Americans and Latinos. This chapter begins to answer this question by examining how the descriptive representation of minorities has changed over time. The next section outlines the history of African-American and Latino representation in the U.S. House in order to place gains made under the Voting Rights Act since 1965 in their proper context. Past levels of representation provide a yardstick against which later advances can be judged.

The chapter then turns to a detailed examination of minority representation in the post–Voting Rights Act era. After tracing the dramatic rise in the number of African-American and Latino representatives and majority-minority districts, the discussion focuses on the connection between racial redistricting and the election of minority officials. The analysis establishes that the well-known link between majority-minority districts and minority representation remains strong despite recent victories by a small number of minority candidates in majority white constituencies. This section further explores the effectiveness of the Voting Rights Act as a tool to force the creation of more majority-minority districts. African Americans and Latinos have not achieved proportional representation in the House of Representatives despite the potency of the act. Battles over the application of the act to redistricting resulted in long delays before the realization of gains due to racial redistricting. Savvy white candidates won election from majority-minority districts and delayed anticipated gains from redistricting. Comparatively low levels of participation among Latinos hamper efforts by Latino candidates to win election from Latino majority districts. The strategy of utilizing racial redistricting to boost the number of minority congressional representatives achieved full flower only during the 1990 redistricting cycle.

The chapter concludes with a discussion of potential costs to African Americans and Latinos of increasing minority representation through racial redistricting. Racial redistricting concentrates African Americans and Latinos into separate majority-minority districts. This policy may have concrete costs for minorities in terms of the loss of congressional clout. Minorities relinquish the opportunity to influence several representatives in exchange for solid control over one representative.

Black and Latino Representation Prior
to the Voting Rights Act

The story of minority representation in the halls of Congress did not begin
with the enactment of the Voting Rights Act of 1965. African Americans involved themselves in the political process and elected several blacks to Congress as soon as the Civil War brought an end to slavery. This brief burst of
black representation quickly faded thanks to repression by southern whites
and a lack of support by northern whites. Latinos won no representation in
Congress until after the turn of the century. Besides demonstrating the in-
voluntary nature of minority political disengagement, the history of minority
representation in Congress provides a baseline to measure increases in minority representation against in the post-Voting Rights Act era.

African-American Representation, 1865–1964

RECONSTRUCTION AND REPRESSION

African Americans first tasted political power during Reconstruction. Republicans encouraged African Americans, strongly supportive of the party of
Lincoln, to vote as a means of maintaining Republican political control of
the South. Reflecting this partisan divide, all Reconstruction-era black congressmen sat in the House as Republicans. The number of blacks elected to
Congress climbed continuously to a peak of eight from 1868 through the
1874 elections.

African-American congressional representation declined by 50 percent to
four in 1876 with the close of Reconstruction. Only one African American
won election to the House in 1888 but blacks did not completely disappear
from the halls of Congress until 1901.[1] African Americans could not successfully resist efforts by so-called redeemers to exclude blacks from the franchise without the support of the federal government. White supremacists
engaged in a variety of legal and state constitutional subterfuges, such as
white primaries, literacy tests, poll taxes, and grandfather clauses, to deny
blacks, and many poor whites, access to the ballot. The threat and the actual
use of violence accompanied by economic intimidation continued to prevent
southern blacks from registering to vote in large numbers until the passage
of the Voting Rights Act of 1965.[2]

No African Americans served in Congress between 1902 and 1928. The
election of Republican Oscar DePriest of Chicago to the House ended the
long drought in black representation. Black membership in the House rose
only to three prior to the onset of the civil rights movement in the late 1950s.
In contrast to nineteenth-century black representatives, who uniformly
hailed from the South, the second wave of black members of Congress represented northern districts located in either Chicago, Detroit, or New York.[3]

The high concentration of blacks in compact areas of each of these cities made it impossible to eliminate these majority black districts without placing large numbers of blacks in neighboring white ethnic constituencies. Black Democrat Arthur Mitchell's defeat of DePriest in 1934 heralded the massive shift in the allegiance of black voters from the Republicans to the Democrats.[4] The attraction of the New Deal overcame old ties to the party of Lincoln. No African American again sat as a Republican in the House until Gary Franks's election in 1990.[5]

RACIAL GERRYMANDERING IN THE NINETEENTH CENTURY

Twenty blacks won forty-one congressional elections between 1868 and 1900. No African American won election from a district with a clear white majority during the nineteenth century. Thirty-six, or 88 percent, of black victories occurred in districts greater than 55 percent black. Florida elected Josiah T. Walls to the House twice in statewide elections though blacks composed only 49 percent of the population. Walls won a single term from a district between 50 and 55 percent black as did Alabaman James T. Rapier and Georgian Jefferson F. Long.[6]

Far from being invented by overzealous civil rights advocates, nineteenth-century southern Democrats enacted the original racial gerrymanders. In the 1870s and 1880s, Alabama, Mississippi, North Carolina, South Carolina, and Virginia adopted racial gerrymanders designed to pack black voters into one congressional district in order to minimize Republican voting strength. Table 2.1 shows the racial composition of congressional districts in these states before and after the adoption of Democratic gerrymanders. The sizable black population explains why Democrats attempted to pack black voters into one district rather than submerge blacks in white majorities in all districts. African Americans formed the majority of the population in Louisiana, Mississippi, and South Carolina and between 45 and 50 percent of the population in Alabama, Florida, and Georgia in 1870. Blacks composed 42 percent of the population in Virginia and 37 percent in North Carolina.

Democratic gerrymanders played an important role in the disfranchisement movement of the 1890s. Preventing the election of more than a few African Americans or Republicans to Congress assured that few southern representatives would protest the exclusion of blacks from the franchise.[7] Several of these early racial gerrymanders that limited black representation somewhat resemble districts drawn during the 1990 redistricting round in order to advance black representation. The Great Migration of blacks from the South to the North along with the migration of whites to the southern states greatly reduced the black share of the population in all southern states over the last century. Plans similar to ones that wasted black votes in the nineteenth century make possible the election of black representa-

TABLE 2.1
Percent Black in Districts of States with Racial Gerrymanders in the Late-Nineteenth Century

State	Gerrymander Type	Year	District									
			1	2	3	4	5	6	7	8	9	10
Alabama		1873–77	57	44	35	51	23	26	41*	41*		
	Democratic	1877–83	54	45	31	65	36	44	20	36		
	Democratic	1883–93	55	50	55	81	43	44	21	36		
Mississippi	Republican	1869–73	48	49	53	63	58					
	Democratic	1873–77	22	56	59	57	56	54				
	Democratic	1877–83	45	53	41	52	52	78				
	Democratic	1883–93	49	54	80	54	52	53	65			
North Carolina		1867–73	50	45	40	43	28	25	12			
	Democratic	1873–83	45	58	42	43	32	36	18	13		
	Democratic	1883–85	47	61	45	45	33	36	18	12	38*	
	Democratic	1885–93	45	63	44	42	39	44	22	16	11	
South Carolina	strange lines	1873–75	61	70	59	46	59*					
		1875–83	60	65	52	51	68					
	Democratic	1883–93	55	63	52	52	55	58	83			
	Democratic	1893–95	38	64	51	54	55	55	81			
Virginia		1869–73	56	51	52	52	46	21	48	15	14	
	Democratic	1873–83	49	52	50	63	38	43	30	36	15	13*
	Democratic	1883–85	48	55	49	65	38	43	29	36	12	
	Democratic	1885–93	51	54	49	65	33	47	26	42		39

Sources: Stanley B. Parsons, William W. Beach, and Michael J. Dubin, *United States Congressional Districts and Data, 1843–1883* (New York: Greenwood Press, 1986); Stanley B. Parsons, Michael J. Dubin, and Karen Toombs Parsons, *United States Congressional Districts, 1883–1913* (New York: Greenwood Press, 1990); "The New Congressional Districts," *Charleston News and Courier*, 6 July 1882, 1.

Note: * signifies an at-large district. South Carolina adopted a plan with many split counties and a noncontiguous district from 1883–1895 as part of its effort to pack black voters into a single district that did not include the city of Charleston.

tives from states dominated by whites in the twentieth. Six southern states did not enact racial gerrymanders to limit Republican voting strength. Blacks in Arkansas, Tennessee, and Texas comprised between 26 and 31 percent of the population in the 1870s—smaller shares than any other southern state. None of these states contained districts that were less than 55 percent white. No Republican won election from Georgia after 1872, so Democrats did not bother to gerrymander even though blacks formed 46 percent of the population.

The reliance of Louisiana's Democratic party on corruption to assure victory probably explains why the Pelican State did not enact a Democratic gerrymander. Several parishes greater than 85 percent black reported that more than 100 percent of registered voters cast their ballots for the Democrat even though blacks overwhelmingly preferred the Republicans in the 1888 gubernatorial election.[8] Florida elected its two representives at large until 1874 when it enacted a plan splitting the state into two districts in which neither blacks nor whites composed more than 55 percent of the population. Due to the dispersion of the black population, it probably would have been difficult to make one district greater than 55 percent black.

Latino Representation, 1865–1964

Prior to the adoption of the Voting Rights Act, very few Latinos won election to Congress. Only one Latino, California Republican Romualdo Pacheco, served in the House before 1912. Except for New Mexico and Louisiana, no states sent Latinos to Congress between 1912 and 1960. Democrat Dennis Chaves, one of the two Latinos ever to hold a Senate seat, represented New Mexico in the Senate from 1935 to 1962.[9]

Black and Latino Representation in the Post–Voting Rights Act Era

African Americans and Latinos have made substantial inroads in congressional representation since the adoption of the Voting Rights Act of 1965. Increases in the number of majority-minority districts under the aegis of the Voting Rights Act explain most of these gains. Neither blacks nor Latinos have achieved representation in the House proportionate to their respective shares of the voting or total population despite these substantial gains. These increases in the number of elected officials did not occur immediately or automatically after the passage of the Voting Rights Act. As will be seen, it was necessary for African Americans and Latinos to utilize legal and legislative strategies in order to firmly establish protection against vote dilution under the Voting Rights Act.

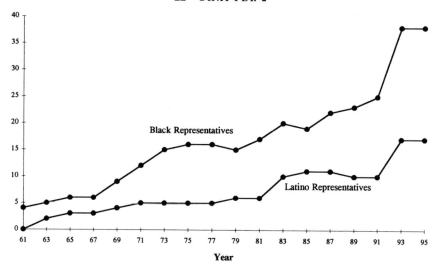

2.1. Number of Black and Latino Representatives. Figure excludes representatives appointed or elected at special elections during a Congress.

Sources: Colleen McGuiness, ed., *American Leaders 1789–1991* (Washington, D.C.: Congressional Quarterly, 1991); Phil Duncan, ed., *Politics in America*, various editions (Washington, D.C.: Congressional Quarterly).

The Second Reconstruction, 1965–1994

Since the passage of the Voting Rights Act, the number of Latino and African-American representatives has steadily increased. Figure 2.1 shows the number of blacks and Latinos elected at the beginning of each Congress. The Eighty-Ninth Congress, which adopted the Voting Rights Act of 1965, contained only five blacks and three Latinos. Voters sent thirty-eight African Americans and seventeen Latinos to Congress in 1992 and 1994, a sixfold jump in the number of Latinos and a sevenfold increase in the number of blacks.[10]

Figure 2.2 plots the number of Latino representatives for each Latino subgroup. Mexican Americans have overwhelmingly dominated the Congressional Hispanic Caucus. New York sent Puerto Rican Herman Badillo, the first non-Mexican Latino elected to Congress, in 1970. The first Cuban-American, Ileana Ros-Lehtinen, entered the House after winning a 1989 special election in Florida.[11] Only after the creation of new majority-minority districts during the 1990 redistricting round did the number of Puerto Rican and Cuban-American representatives rise above one apiece. Three Puerto Ricans, two from New York and one from Chicago, and three Cuban Americans, two from Miami and one from New Jersey, gained election to the House in 1992 and 1994.[12]

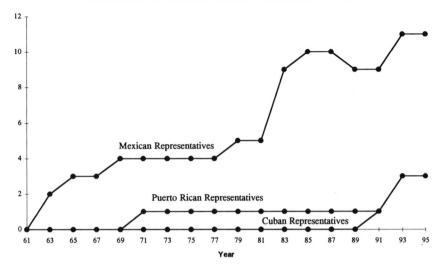

2.2. Number of Mexican, Puerto Rican, and Cuban Representatives. Figure excludes representatives appointed or elected at special elections during a Congress.
  Sources: McGuiness, *American Leaders 1789–1991*; Duncan, *Politics in America*, various
editions.

The Link between Descriptive Representation and
Majority-Minority Districts

The growth in the number of black and Latino representatives closely
tracks the rise in the number of black and Latino majority districts. Except
for a sharp increase in the general redistricting following the 1990 census,
the number of black and Latino majority districts generally increased gradually (see figs. 2.3 and 2.4). Only six members represented black majority
districts in 1961. States drew seventeen black majority districts by 1985.
The number of black majority districts jumped to thirty-two in the wake
of the 1990 redistricting round. Similarly, the number of Latino majority
districts rose from three in 1973 to nine in 1983.[13] The number of representatives hailing from Latino majority districts more than doubled in 1993,
rising to nineteen.

  Random chance does not account for the close relationship between the
drawing of majority-minority districts and the election of minority representatives. As the following chapter reveals, Latinos and blacks rarely win in
majority white districts. Tables 2.2 and 2.3 list the African Americans and
Latinos serving in the House of Representatives in 1996. Thirty-one of the
thirty-eight black members of the House represent majority black districts.
Five of the remaining seven won election from majority-minority districts.
Latinos usually comprise most of the nonblack minority portion of the

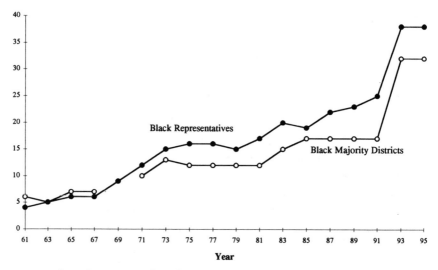

2.3. Number of Districts with a Black Majority or a Black Representative. Figure excludes representatives appointed or elected at special eleactions during a Congress. Data on black majority districts unavailable for 1969–1970.

Sources: Data on black representatives from McGuiness, *American Leaders, 1789–1991; Politics in America,* various editions. Data on black majority districts from the following Bureau of the Census publications: *Congressional District Data Book (Districts of the 87th Congress),* Table 1, Items 1, 7; *Congressional District Data Book (Districts of the 88th Congress and Supplements),* Items 29, 40; *Congressional District Data Book—93d Congress, 94th Congress,* Items 18, 40; *1980 Census of Population and Housing: Congressional Districts of the 98th Congress and Supplements,* Table 1; *1990 Census of Population and Housing: Population and Housing Characteristics of the 103rd Congress,* Table 1.

population.[14] Only Republicans Gary Franks of Connecticut and J.C. Watts of Oklahoma represent mostly white districts. Recent high-profile victories by black candidates like Illinois Senator Carol Moseley-Braun, Virginia Governor Doug Wilder, and Dallas Mayor Ron Kirk in white majority constituencies have led some scholars to contend that blacks no longer require black majority districts to guarantee black representation.[15] Unfortunately, these observers base their argument virtually entirely on anecdotal evidence. The vast majority of African-American members of Congress win election from black majority districts. Except for Republicans Gary Franks and J.C. Watts, blacks represent black majority districts and whites represent white majority districts.

Latinos represent majority-minority districts with no exceptions. Only two Latino representatives do not hail from Latino majority constituencies. New Jersey Democrat Robert Menendez represents a 40 percent Latino and 13 percent black district. New Mexico Democrat Bill Richardson serves a constituency in which Latinos and American Indians together constitute a

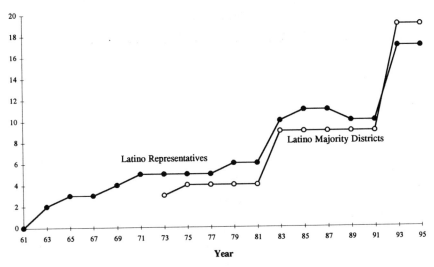

2.4. Number of Districts with a Latino Majority or a Latino Representative. Figure excludes representatives appointed or elected at special elections during a Congress. Data on Latino majority districts unavailable prior to 1973.

Sources: Data on Latino representatives from McGuiness, American Leaders, 1789–1991; Duncan, Politics in America, various editions. Data on Latino majority districts from the following Bureau of the Census publications: Congressional District Data Book—93d Congress, 94th Congress, Items 18, 50A; 1980 Census of Population and Housing: Congressional Districts of the 98th Congress and Supplements, Table 1; 1990 Census of Population and Housing: Population and Housing Characteristics of the 103rd Congress, Table 1.

majority. African Americans invariably represent majority-minority districts in which neither blacks nor Latinos separately form a majority even when Latinos outnumber blacks. Low rates of electoral participation among Latinos explain black success in these heterogeneous majority-minority districts.

Percentage of the House versus Percentage
in the Population

Blacks and Latinos have not yet achieved proportional representation despite the massive increase in the number of blacks and Latinos in the 1992 congressional elections. Figure 2.5 shows changes over time in the ratio of the percentage of blacks in the House and the percentage of black majority districts to the percentage of blacks in the general population. Figure 2.6 displays the equivalent information for Latinos. The ratio between percentage in the House and percentage in the general population would equal one if blacks or Latinos had attained exact proportional representation. Neither blacks nor Latinos have ever come close to winning proportional representation, so the ratio has always been below one.

TABLE 2.2
African-American Representatives in 1996

Name	District	Percent Black	Percent Latino	Percent Minority
Major Owens	NY 11	74.0%	11.5%	88.7%
Elijah Cummings	MD 07	71.0	0.9	73.5
Barbara-Rose Collins	MI 15	70.0	4.3	75.4
Bobby Rush	IL 01	69.7	3.6	74.4
John Conyers	MI 14	69.1	1.1	71.5
Jesse Jackson, Jr.	IL 02	68.5	6.6	75.8
Earl Hilliard	AL 07	67.5	0.3	68.1
Cardiss Collins	IL 07	65.6	4.3	73.2
Robert Scott	VA 03	64.4	1.3	67.1
Cynthia McKinney	GA 11	64.1	1.0	65.9
Bennie Thompson	MS 02	63.0	0.5	63.9
John Lewis	GA 05	62.3	1.8	65.1
James Clyburn	SC 06	62.3	0.5	63.1
Chaka Fattah	PA 02	62.2	1.6	66.3
William Jefferson	LA 02	61.1	3.4	66.5
Edolphus Towns	NY 10	60.7	19.7	83.1
Donald Payne	NJ 10	60.2	12.3	75.2
Harold Ford	TN 09	59.2	0.7	60.8
Louis Stokes	OH 11	58.6	1.1	60.9
Albert Wynn	MD 04	58.5	6.4	69.8
Cleo Fields	LA 04	58.5	1.1	60.2
Carrie Meek	FL 17	58.4	23.0	82.9
Eva Clayton	NC 01	57.3	0.7	58.8
Melvin Watt	NC 12	56.6	0.9	58.8
Sanford Bishop	GA 02	56.5	1.5	58.5
Floyd Flake	NY 06	56.2	16.9	80.0
Corrine Brown	FL 03	55.0	2.8	58.9
William Clay	MO 01	52.3	0.9	54.4
Alcee Hastings	FL 23	51.6	9.4	62.1
Sheila Jackson-Lee	TX 18	50.9	15.3	69.4
Eddie Bernice Johnson	TX 30	50.0	17.1	69.5
Charles Rangel	NY 15	46.9	46.4	96.4
Maxine Waters	CA 35	42.7	43.1	92.2
Julian Dixon	CA 32	40.3	30.2	78.8
Juanita Millender-McDonald	CA 37	33.6	45.1	90.0
Ronald Dellums	CA 09	31.8	12.0	60.1
J.C. Watts	OK 04	7.1	3.9	17.2
Gary Franks	CT 05	4.8	6.2	12.6

Sources: Clark Bensen, *Polidata Election Reports: Congressional Districts, 103rd Congress* (Lake Ridge, Virginia: Polidata, 1993); Phil Duncan and Christine Lawrence, eds., *Politics in America 1996* (Washington, D.C.: Congressional Quarterly, 1995); *1990 U.S. Census of Population and Housing: 104th Congress: Congressional Districts of the United States, Summary Tape File 1D, Summary Tape File 4D* (CD-ROM).

Note: Percent Black is the percentage of blacks in the total population. Percent Latino is the percentage of Hispanics in the total population. Percent Minority is the percentage in the total population who are not non-Hispanic whites.

TABLE 2.3
Latino Representatives in 1996

Name	District	Percent Latino	Percent Black	Percent Minority
Lucille Roybal-Allard	CA 33	83.7	4.5	93.1
E. "Kika" de la Garza	TX 15	74.5	1.1	76.1
Lincoln Diaz-Balart	FL 21	69.6	4.1	75.3
Ileana Ros-Lehtinen	FL 18	66.7	4.2	72.2
Solomon P. Ortiz	TX 27	66.2	2.4	69.5
Luis V. Gutierrez	IL 04	65.0	6.3	74.3
Henry Bonilla	TX 23	62.5	2.9	66.5
Esteban E. Torres	CA 34	62.3	1.9	74.1
Xavier Becerra	CA 30	61.5	3.5	86.8
Henry B. Gonzalez	TX 20	60.7	5.8	68.2
Frank Tejeda	TX 28	60.4	8.5	69.9
Jose E. Serrano	NY 16	60.2	42.2	99.9
Matthew G. Martinez	CA 31	58.5	1.7	83.5
Nydia M. Velázquez	NY 12	57.9	13.7	91.8
Ed Pastor	AZ 02	50.5	6.8	63.1
Robert Menendez	NJ 13	41.5	13.7	60.1
Bill Richardson	NM 03	34.6	1.2	56.5

Sources: Clark Benson, *Polidata Election Reports: Congressional Districts, 103rd Congress* (Lake Ridge, Virginia: Polidata, 1993); Phil Duncan and Christine Lawrence, eds., *Politics in America 1996* (Washington, D.C.: Congressional Quarterly, 1995).

Note: Percent Latino is the percentage of Hispanics in the total population. Percent Black is the percentage of blacks in the total population. Percent Minority is the percentage of the total population who are not non-Hispanic whites.

African Americans have made more progress toward gaining the number of seats corresponding to their share of the population than Latinos. African Americans won only 9 percent of the seats that they would have won if the percentage of black victories had equalled the percentage of blacks in the population in 1960. Thanks to a huge increase in the number of majority black districts, that figure rose to just over 73 percent in the 1992 and 1994 elections. Increases in the ratio of seats to population for Latinos lag relative to the rise in African-American representation. No Latinos won election to Congress in 1960, so the ratio was the lowest possible at zero. The rate of increase in the seats-population ratio for Latinos has been fairly steady since the 1970s. Latinos gained 43 percent of the seats they would have won if their representation had been proportionate in the 1992 and 1994 elections. The ratio of seats to population fell slightly behind the ratio of Latino majority districts to population for the first time in 1992 due to white victories in Latino majority districts.[16]

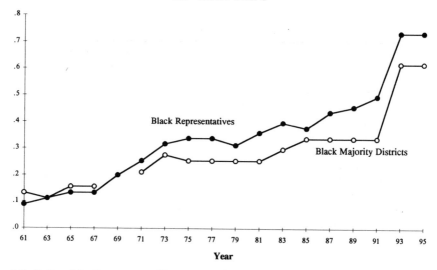

2.5. Ratio of the Percentage of Districts with a Black Majority or a Black Representative to the Percentage of Blacks. Figure excludes representatives appointed or elected at special elections during a Congress. Data on black majority districts unavailable for 1969–1970.

Sources: Data on black representatives from McGuiness, *American Leaders, 1789–1991*; Duncan, *Politics in America*, various editions. Data on black majority districts from the following Bureau of the Census publications: *Congressional District Data Book (Districts of the 87th Congress)*, Table 1, Items 1, 7; *Congressional District Data Book (Districts of the 88th Congress and Supplements)*, Items 29, 40; *Congressional District Data Book—93d Congress, 94th Congress*, Items 18, 40; *1980 Census of Population and Housing: Congressional Districts of the 98th Congress and Supplements*, Table 1; *1990 Census of Population and Housing: Population and Housing Characteristics of the 103rd Congress*, Table 1.

Why Did Minority Descriptive Representation
Take So Long to Achieve?

Building the Legal Basis for Drawing Majority-Minority
Districts, 1965–1986

The strategy of drawing new majority black and Latino districts to promote the election of members of these groups culminated in the the creation of many new majority-minority districts during the 1990 redistricting round. Sections 2 and 5 of the Voting Rights Act underpinned this strategy. The Justice Department used its power under Section 5 to deny preclearance to force states to draw new majority-minority districts.[17] Section 2 made it possible to file suit to prevent redistricting plans that would reduce minority representation from going into effect. The Supreme Court's 1976 adoption of the "no retrogression" standard in *Beer v. United States* effectively made it illegal to eliminate black congressional districts.

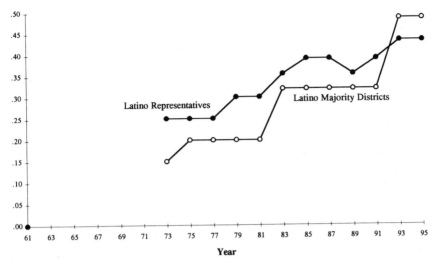

2.6. Ratio of the Percentage of Districts with a Latino Majority or a Latino Representative to the Percentage of Latinos. Figure excludes representatives appointed or
elected at special elections during a Congress. Data on Latino majority districts unavailable prior to 1973.
Sources: Data on Latino representatives from McGuiness, *American Leaders, 1789–1991*;
Duncan, *Politics in America*, various editions. Data on Latino majority districts from the following Bureau of the Census publications: *Congressional District Data Book—93d Congress, 94th
Congress*, Items 18, 50A; *1980 Census of Population and Housing: Congressional Districts of the
98th Congress and Supplements*, Table 1; *1990 Census of Population and Housing: Population
and Housing Characteristics of the 103rd Congress*, Table 1.

State legislators protected existing majority-minority districts and created
new ones under threat of having their work undone by the Justice Department or the judiciary. African Americans represented ten of the fourteen
congressional districts that lost more than 10 percent of their population between 1980 and 1990.[18] The new maps carefully preserved black dominance
in these districts despite these population losses in order to receive preclearance as required under Section 5 from the Justice Department and avoid
lawsuits claiming vote dilution under Section 2.

The Voting Rights Act resulted in steady, incremental change in the number of black and Latino majority districts in the two decades following its enactment in 1965, but the full application of the act to redistricting arrived
only in 1990. Several factors account for this delay. Implementation of the
act in its initial phase rightly focused on the fundamental problem of low levels of black voter registration in the South. Several states eliminated existing
black majority electoral constituencies in an effort to thwart the efforts of
new black voters to elect black officials.[19]

Several decades of legislative and legal wrangling passed before Congress
and the courts made clear that the Voting Rights Act applied to redistricting

plans regardless of whether the mapmakers intended to discriminate. The Supreme Court upheld the constitutionality of the major sections of the act in *South Carolina v. Katzenbach* in 1966, and the Court ruled that Section 5 applied to redistricting in *Allen v. State Board of Elections* in 1969. Congress extended coverage of the Voting Rights Act to include language minorities, including Latinos and American Indians, in 1975.[20] The Court did not firmly establish the right to file suit against vote dilution under Section 2's antidiscrimination provisions until 1977 in *Kirksey v. Board of Supervisors of Hinds County*. In a major setback for proponents of racial redistricting, the Court stated in *Mobile v. Bolden* in 1980 that litigants in vote dilution cases need to provide evidence of intentional discrimination to win cases claiming vote dilution in redistricting. Congress specifically overturned this decision when renewing the Voting Rights Act in 1982, and replaced the intent standard with the effect standard outlined by the judiciary in *White v. Regester* and *Zimmer v. McKeithen*. Through its 1986 decision in *Thornburg v. Gingles*, the Supreme Court upheld the 1982 amendments and made it much easier to prove claims of vote dilution and force states to draw majority-minority districts.

Until 1990, the Department of Justice concentrated more on the preservation of existing majority-minority districts than on the creation of new ones, in line with the Supreme Court's 1976 decision in *Beer v. United States* favoring "no retrogression" over requiring maximizing minority representation. *Thornburg v. Gingles* paved the way for minorities, the Department of Justice, and Republicans to successfully press state legislators to create new majority-minority constituencies during the 1990 redistricting cycle with the full force of the Voting Rights Act behind them.[21] Judges undertook the job of drawing districts favorable to the election of blacks and Latinos when state legislators could not agree on a redistricting plan or the courts declared a state legislative plan invalid. Fourteen states created at least one new majority black or Latino congressional district.

Whites Continue to Win Some Majority-Minority Districts

Not all new majority-minority districts immediately elected a black or Latino to Congress. Many non-Hispanic whites retired or sought reelection elsewhere after their constituencies became majority minority, but six black majority and seven Latino majority districts continued to send whites to the House for at least a period of time. Tables 2.4 and 2.5 list these districts and describe the political situation in each district that led to the continued election of whites to Congress from predominantly minority districts. Except for one case, white incumbents continued to win in black districts due to strong support from African Americans. Whites often win Latino districts because of low levels of registration and voting among Latinos.

TABLE 2.4
Black Majority Districts Won by Whites

District	Location	Created	First Black	Years Delay
Georgia 05	Atlanta	1982	1986	6

When 56% white, this district elected black Democrat Andrew Young in 1972, 1974, and 1976. After Young became U.N. Ambassador, liberal white Democrat Wyche Fowler won a special election to replace Young and easily held the district when it became 65% black in 1982. Under pressure to vacate the seat for an African American, Fowler successfully ran for the Senate in 1986. Civil rights leader John Lewis has held the seat since.

District	Location	Created	First Black	Years Delay
Louisiana 02	New Orleans	1984	1990	6

White liberal Democratic incumbent Lindy Boggs had little trouble holding this seat even after it became 59% black in 1984. Black Democrat William Jefferson won the election to replace Boggs in 1990 after her voluntary retirement.

District	Location	Created	First Black	Years Delay
Mississippi 02	Delta Region	1982	1986	4

Black Democrat Robert Clark failed to defeat white Republican Webb Franklin in this racially polarized district in 1982 when it was 54% black or 1984 when the black percentage was raised to 56%. Though blacks formed a majority of the district's population, they did not always form a majority of the electorate. Mike Espy, who ran a strong get-out-the-vote campaign among blacks and was more acceptable to whites, defeated Franklin in 1986. Redistricting increased the percentage of blacks to 63% prior to the 1992 election. African-American Democrat Bennie Thompson won a special election to replace Espy in 1993.

District	Location	Created	First Black	Years Delay
New Jersey 10	Newark	1972	1988	16

Italian-American Peter Rodino protected civil rights legislation from attack from his position as chairman of the Judiciary Committee, throughout the Reagan era and gained strong black support in this 56% black district. Even Jesse Jackson's endorsement did not enable black Donald Payne, Rodino's eventual successor, to defeat the incumbent in 1986. Under pressure to vacate the seat for a black, Rodino retired in 1988.

District	Location	Created	First Black	Years Delay
New York 06	Queens	1982	1986	4

White incumbent Democrat Joe Addabbo held this 50% black and 9% Latino district until he died in 1986 through aggressive campaigning. Democrat Floyd Flake lost the special election primary to another black candidate, but he won the regular election primary and has held the seat since.

District	Location	Created	First Black	Years Delay
Pennsylvania 01	Philadelphia	1992		?

Incumbent Democrat Thomas Foglietta easily won reelection from this 52% black and 10% Latino district in 1992 and 1994. Challenged for the Democratic nomination in 1994 by an African-American former television reporter, Foglietta won with 69% of the vote.

TABLE 2.5
Latino Majority Districts Won by Whites

District	Location	Created	First Latino	Years Delay
California 20	Fresno	1992		?

White incumbent Democrat Calvin Dooley had little trouble holding this 55% Latino, 6% black, and 5% Asian district in 1992 or 1994. Latinos and Asians in the district register and vote at low rates.

District	Location	Created	First Latino	Years Delay
California 26	San Fernando Valley	1992		?

White incumbent Democrat Howard Berman easily won reelection in 1992 and 1994 from this 52% Latino, 4% black district in which Latino turnout is low.

District	Location	Created	First Latino	Years Delay
Florida 18	Miami	1982	1989	17

Unswerving opposition to the Castro regime combined with the devotion of his elderly constituents helped Claude Pepper hold this district until his death even though the district was 51% Latino, mostly Cuban, and 16% black in 1982. The black-Cuban divide undoubtedly aided Pepper by preventing the formation of a coalition of minorities in this district. Republican Ileana Ros-Lehtinen became the first Cuban elected to Congress in 1989. Redistricting increased the percentage of Latinos to 67% prior to the 1992 election.

District	Location	Created	First Latino	Years Delay
Texas 16	El Paso	1972		?

White incumbent Ronald Coleman's 673 overdrafts caused him more problems than his ethnicity in 1992 when he nearly lost to a white Republican in the general election. Coleman easily defeated his Mexican primary opponent in 1992 and his Mexican general election opponent in 1994 despite the increase in the district's Latino percentage to 70% in 1992 from 60% in 1982. From 1964 until 1982, white Richard White represented the district, which became 50% Latino in 1972.

District	Location	Created	First Latino	Years Delay
Texas 23	San Antonio	1982	1984	2

Albert Bustamante ousted incumbent Abraham Kazam in the 1984 Democratic primary, one term after redistricting made the district 56% Latino. Republican Henry Bonilla defeated Bustamante for reelection in 1992.

District	Location	Created	First Latino	Years Delay
Texas 29	Houston	1992		?

White Democrat Gene Green won this district tailored to elect a Latino. Green defeated Mexican Ben Reyes in the Democratic primary in 1992 and 1994 despite the district's 61% Latino majority and 10% black population. Low levels of turnout in the Latino community combined with a lack of cohesion among the district's diverse Latino population contributed to Green's victories.

BLACK MAJORITY DISTRICTS

Whites who worked aggressively to earn black votes through diligent constituency service and dedication to protecting the interests of the black community account for five of the six cases of black majority districts won by whites. New Jersey Representative Peter Rodino, chairman of the House Judiciary Committee, staunchly advocated civil rights. Lindy Boggs strongly supported social programs that benefited many district residents and made herself accessible to black constituents by holding office hours in housing projects.[22]

Black candidates invariably win the open black majority seats when white incumbents retire from the House. Pressure from black leaders to make way for a black representative sometimes contributes to the decision by white incumbents to step down. During his 1986 campaign for reelection, Rodino promised, much to his later regret, that he would retire after serving one last term. Georgian Wyche Fowler received strong encouragement to seek election to the Senate, rather than reelection to the House, in 1986. Robin Tallon of South Carolina retired and Tom McMillen of Maryland switched districts after facing opposition to their seeking reelection from newly created black majority districts in 1992. Unsurprisingly, many black politicians wanted to represent these districts and feared battling against the resources usually commanded by entrenched incumbents. White Democrats anxious to maintain racial harmony within their party further discouraged white incumbents from seeking reelection in black districts. Democrat Thomas Foglietta is currently the only white to represent a black majority district.

The Second District of Mississippi, won by white Republican Webb Franklin in 1982 and 1984, forms the sole exception to this pattern. Even after boundary changes increased the black voting-age population from 48 to 53 percent in 1984, whites outnumbered blacks at the polls due to differing levels of voter turnout. Black Democrat Mike Espy won the district in 1986 by mobilizing the black vote and conciliating whites. After his initial election with 52 percent of the vote, Espy coasted to victory with 65 percent in 1988, and 84 percent in 1990 because he received an increasingly large share of the white vote. African-American Bennie Thompson won a special election to replace Espy in 1993 after Espy's appointment as Secretary of Agriculture. Thompson has made little effort to woo white voters and has had more anemic vote totals as a result. Thompson won the open seat with 55 percent of the vote in 1993, and garnered only 54 percent of ballots cast in 1994.

In contrast to black majority districts, successful white candidates in Latino majority districts owe their victories largely to inordinately low levels of voter registration and turnout among Latinos. Latinos often compose a far lower proportion of the electorate than in the general population. According to the Latino National Political Survey, voter participation rates differ substantially between Latinos and non-Latinos and among Latinos by national origin. While 61 percent of whites voted for Congress in 1988, only 39 percent of Mexican Americans and 31 percent of Puerto Ricans cast ballots. At 54 percent, Cuban Americans participated at a markedly higher rate, but still voted at a lower rate than whites.[23] Many Latino majority population districts simply do not have majority Latino electorates.

White representatives of Latino districts do not inherently ignore Latino concerns. Claude Pepper received national attention for his devotion to elderly issues toward the end of his career, but his strong anti-Castro and pro-Israel stands undoubtedly reflected the views of his Cuban and Jewish constituents. Low levels of voting can result in more dubious representation. Republican Bob Dornan's right-wing views satisfy the Republican electoral majority in his California district but probably clash with the opinions held by the Latino and black majority in his district.

Potential Costs of Racial Redistricting

The number of African Americans and Latinos represented by whites has declined with the election of minority representatives from new majority-minority districts. African Americans and Latinos who believe that white representation has been unresponsive and want to see members of their own group advance may not lament this change. However, blacks and Latinos may lose influence over the policy-making process by concentrating their votes in only a few minority controlled congressional districts.

Drawing Majority-Minority Districts Requires Separating People by Race

The Voting Rights Act perplexingly integrates the Congress by separating people into different congressional districts on the basis of race. The high degree of racial segregation in society as a whole makes placing minorities into separate congressional districts far easier. Figure 2.7 shows the percentage of African Americans who live in black majority districts or have a black representative. African Americans represented under 5 percent of blacks in

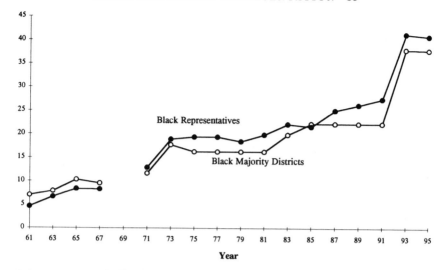

2.7. Percentage of All African Americans Living in Black Majority Districts or with Black Representatives. Figure excludes representatives appointed or elected at special elections during a Congress. Data on black population unavailable for 1969–1970.

Sources: Data on black representatives from McGuiness, *American Leaders, 1789–1991*; Duncan, *Politics in America*, various editions. Data on black majority districts from the following Bureau of the Census publications: *Congressional District Data Book* (Districts of the 87th Congress), Table 1. Items 1,7; *Congressional District Data Book* (Districts of the 88th Congress and Supplements), Items 29, 40; *Congressional District Data Book—93d Congress, 94th Congress*, Items 18, 40; *1980 Census of Population and Housing: Congressional Districts of the 98th Congress and Supplements*, Table 1; *1990 Census of Population and Housing: Population and Housing Characteristics of the 103rd Congress*, Table 1.

1961, but 22 percent by 1983. This statistic shot up to a new high of 41 percent in 1993. The creation of additional black majority districts and the election of new black representatives has raised the proportion of whites living in districts with a black majority or a black representative. Figure 2.8 reveals that the percentage of whites represented by blacks has risen from an infinitesimal .2 percent in 1961 to a still small 4 percent in 1995.

The percentage of Latinos represented by Latinos or living in Latino majority districts has also increased, but not to the degree as among African Americans. Latinos represented only 14 percent of Latinos and a scant 9 percent of Latinos lived in majority Latino districts in 1973. The percentage of Latinos living in Latino majority districts doubled to 19 percent by 1983, though the percentage with a Latino representative rose only four points to 18 percent. As with African Americans, the percentage of Latinos residing in Latino majority districts spiked with the elections following the drawing

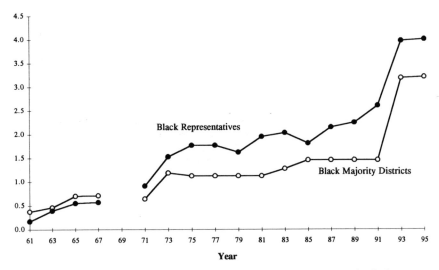

2.8. Percentage of All Whites Living in Black Majority Districts or with Black Representatives. Figure excludes representatives appointed or elected at special elections during a Congress. Data on white population unavailable for 1969–1970.

Sources: Data on black representatives from McGuiness, ed. *American Leaders, 1789–1991*; Duncan, *Politics in America*, various editions. Data on white population and black majority districts from the following Bureau of the Census publications: *Congressional District Data Book (Districts of the 87th Congress)*, Table 1, Items 1, 6, 7; *Congressional District Data Book (Districts of the 88th Congress and Supplements)*, Items 29, 39, 40; *Congressional District Data Book—93d Congress, 94th Congress*, Items 18, 39, 40; *1980 Census of Population and Housing: Congressional Districts of the 98th Congress and Supplements*, Table 1; *1990 Census of Population and Housing: Population and Housing Characteristics of the 103rd Congress*, Table 1.

of many new Latino districts during the 1990 redistricting round. Latino members of Congress currently represent 26 percent of all Latinos and 31 percent of Latinos live in Latino majority districts.

Though racial redistricting has raised the probability of concordance between the race of citizens and their representatives, majority-minority districts are no more likely to be racially homogenous than white districts. All of the new majority-minority districts contain sizable white minorities.[24] Though the number of blacks represented by blacks and of Latinos represented by Latinos has clearly increased, whites still represent around three-quarters of Latinos and nearly 60 percent of African Americans.

Majority-Minority Districts May Cost Blacks and Latinos Influence

Racial redistricting may dishearteningly make minority representatives increasingly symbolic, rather than influential, figures within the House just as their numbers increase. Concentrating minorities into a single congressional district forces them to forgo the opportunity to potentially influence several representatives in majority white districts. Ultimately, as chapter 6 demonstrates, this loss of influence reduces the chances of the House adopting policies favored by minorities. The inability of large numbers of minority representatives to influence public policy could delegitimize the political system and minority leaders who seek public office.

Separating minority officials into majority-minority congressional districts may further prevent these officials from building up a sufficient political base among whites to run for higher offices, such as senator or governor. Demonstrating an ability to represent whites on a lower level of government may aid minority officials who wish to gain white support for a bid to higher office. Majority-minority districts may alternatively provide minority candidates with the political base and experience needed to launch credible challenges for statewide office. Doug Wilder represented a black majority district in the Virginia Senate prior to his successful bids for lieutenant governor and governor.

Even if minorities can influence the policy process through the election of white representatives, a question analyzed in later chapters, the election of blacks and Latinos contributes to the political process in other ways. The election of African Americans and Latinos to Congress legitimates the political process for members of these previously powerless and excluded groups. Electing some of its members to positions of authority empowers members of any group because the very existence of minority representatives provides direct evidence that members of such groups can influence the choice of elected officials and participate actively in the political arena. Concerns over the potential loss of substantive representation should not cause observers to quickly dismiss the value of symbolic representation.

The strong arguments on both sides of this debate highlight the need for more empirical analysis to answer the question of what factors influence the election of minorities and how different districting plans influence public policy outcomes. Later chapters should help shed light on these questions. The answers will hopefully inform and improve the debate over racial redistricting, so that policymakers can make decisions regarding race and representation knowing, rather than intuiting, the effect of various districting plans on the election of African-American and Latino representatives and their public policy interests.

Conclusion

The Voting Rights Act of 1965 has enhanced African-American and Latino descriptive representation a great deal. Legal and congressional battles over the application of the act to redistricting slowed the creation of new majority-minority districts. Once these districts were created, the ability of white incumbents to continue winning even in those in which blacks make up a majority temporarily held off the election of black representatives in some instances. Low registration and turnout among Latinos has made it more difficult for Latinos to win Latino majority districts. The number of African Americans and Latinos elected to Congress has soared despite these barriers. The racial redistricting strategy culminated in the creation of record numbers of majority-minority districts and the election of substantial numbers of new African-American and Latino representatives in 1992. Neither blacks nor Latinos have achieved representation proportionate to their share of the voting or total population. Racial redistricting may also cost minorities much-needed influence over white representatives. Later chapters explore this crucial question of whether racial redistricting reduces the substantive representation of black and Latino interests in Congress.

3

THE ELECTION OF BLACK AND

LATINO REPRESENTATIVES

THE JUSTIFICATION for the creation of majority-minority districts rests on the claim that whites almost never vote for minority candidates in sufficient numbers to elect a black or Latino candidate from a white majority district. Majority-minority districts remain essential to the election of more than token numbers of African Americans and Latinos according to advocates of racial redistricting. They fear that the Supreme Court's decisions in *Shaw v. Reno* and *Miller v. Johnson* will result in fewer majority-minority districts with disastrous consequences for descriptive representation.

Opponents of racial redistricting vocally disagree. Racism may persist and even make winning election more difficult for blacks and Latinos but it no longer represents an insurmountable barrier to their election in their view. Critics fear that racial redistricting prevents the political integration of America by segregating minorities into separate districts and making it much less likely that minorities will run and win in majority white constituencies.[1]

This line of reasoning suggests that other factors besides race influence whether a district sends a minority representative to Washington. Several nonracial variables seem potentially related to the election of black or Latino representatives. Minorities almost invariably represent urban low-income districts with few highly educated residents. Districts with black and Latino representatives often have a relatively high percentage of foreign-born residents. African Americans represent a disproportionate share of the nation's government workers.

The analysis presented below proves that nonracial demographic variables like education, income, and urbanicity effectively serve as proxies for race. Blacks and Latinos disproportionately represent citizens of low socioeconomic status not because poor whites support the election of minorities at a greater rate than affluent whites, but because African Americans and Latinos lag behind whites on these indicators. The high percentage of urban residents in black and Latino districts does not reflect that whites in urban areas support minority candidates at relatively high rates, but that drawing majority-minority districts is much easier in highly segregated urban centers with large concentrated minority populations than in rural areas with scattered minority populations. Only the percentage of blacks and Latinos in the district alters the probability of an African American winning election to the House. Only the percentage of Latinos and the percentage of citizens affects the chances of a Latino carrying the district.

Opponents of racial redistricting, including the narrow Supreme Court majority in *Shaw v. Reno* and *Miller v. Johnson*, wrongly contend that the role of race in elections has declined and that African Americans and Latinos can now regularly carry white majority districts. Racial redistricting may remain morally unpalatable because it requires that a nation that aspires to racial neutrality in its politics sort people according to race during the re-districting process. Classifying by race violates the sense that government should act in a colorblind fashion and that members of any racial group hold a wide variety of opinions. Residents of congressional districts, how-ever, must elect their representatives as a group. Despite the diversity of opinions within racial groups, racial redistricting remains vital to the elec-tion of the African-American and Latino candidates usually preferred by mi-nority voters.

Past Studies

Political scientists clash over whether significant numbers of blacks and Latinos can win election to the House from majority non-Hispanic white districts. Based on their study of the 1982, 1984 and 1986 elections, Bernard Grofman and Lisa Handley conclude that "black members of Congress are elected from black plurality districts in which combined black plus Hispanic population is above 50%."[2] They have an even gloomier outlook on prospects for Latino representation:

> In general, except in New Mexico and California, Hispanics are not elected to Congress in districts that are less than 63% combined minority (black plus Hispanic). Including California and New Mexico, it would seem that a clear Hispanic plurality and a combined minority population above 55% give a sub-stantial likelihood, although not certainty, of Hispanic success. To achieve ac-tual certainty, a clear Hispanic plurality and a combined minority population near 70% seem necessary.[3]

Much of the literature on the Voting Rights Act simply assumes that racial polarization precludes minorities from winning election in white majority districts.[4]

Abigail Thernstrom forcefully disputes this conventional wisdom. She contends that the Voting Rights Act as written in 1965 was designed solely to assure access to the ballot, not to guarantee the election of blacks to office through racial gerrymandering. Relying exclusively on anecdotal evidence, Thernstrom claims that the racial polarization justifying such measures no longer exists and that blacks who live in white majority districts influence which white candidate wins election and occasionally elect one of their own to office.[5]

Carol Swain makes a pragmatic case for departing from the strategy of drawing majority-minority districts. She points out that the upper limit on black representation from majority black districts is quickly being reached. Legislatures and courts created close to the maximum feasible number of black majority districts during the 1990 redistricting cycle. African Americans won thirty-seven of thirty-eight majority white districts in the 1992 and 1994 congressional elections. White majority districts provide more fertile ground for future black representation according to Swain. She believes that racial redistricting supporters overestimate white racism and ignore breakthrough elections like those of Alan Wheat in Missouri and Doug Wilder in Virginia. Swain readily concedes that African Americans find it harder to win election from majority white districts, but argues that, with a concerted effort, blacks can make substantial gains in them. She fears that concentrating blacks into majority black districts causes African Americans to lose important opportunities to influence the electoral outcome and even elect greater numbers of black representatives in white majority districts.[6]

Swain and Thernstrom's analyses can be extended to Latinos. Whites still represent several Latino majority districts, but these districts could limit Latino representation over the long run. The successful gubernatorial campaigns of Robert Martinez in Florida and Tony Anaya in New Mexico may indicate that Latinos find it easier than blacks to win election in majority white constituencies. Concentrating the Latino vote in predominantly Latino districts may force Latinos to relinquish opportunities to influence elections across district lines.

The remainder of this chapter examines congressional elections from 1972 though 1994 in order to answer the question of whether the election of substantial numbers of minority representatives require the drawing of majority-minority districts. Rather than studying only the racial composition of the district, the analysis includes other district demographic characteristics to assess their influence on the race of the representative compared to race.

Black Representatives

Race Overwhelms All Other Factors

Determining whether blacks hold majority status in a congressional district provides a simple cue for predicting the race of a district's representative. Nonblacks won 5007 of the 5079 elections held in white majority districts between 1972 and 1994; blacks triumphed in 200 of the 219 elections in black majority districts.[7]

Examining elections in which a black candidate carried a white district or vice-versa undermines Swain's and Thernstrom's argument that blacks regularly win election from majority white districts. Eleven representatives from mixed majority-minority districts in which blacks and Latinos together comprise a majority account for forty-five of the seventy-two elections that blacks won in "white" districts.[8]

Six African-American representatives won twenty-seven elections in six genuinely white majority districts. These few elections spark little hope that blacks can frequently win election from majority white districts. The extremely liberal congressional district centered on Berkeley and Oakland, California, has sent Ron Dellums to Congress twelve times.[9] Katie Hall won a special election to represent Gary, Indiana, in the House in 1982 after being appointed to fill a vacancy. Hall successfully sought reelection to a full term later in 1982, but lost her first contested Democratic primary in 1984 even though her two white opponents split the white vote. Hall failed to recapture the Democratic nomination in her 1986 comeback bid.[10]

African Americans won thirteen elections is white districts that cannot so easily be chalked up as anomalies. Missouri Democrat Alan Wheat won six terms from an 80 percent white district before giving up his seat to pursue an unsuccessful senatorial bid in 1994. Wheat emerged victorious from the 1982 Democratic primary for the open seat with 31 percent of the vote—only 1004 votes and 1 percent more than his closest white rival, Kansas City councilman John Carnes. If Missouri held runoff primaries, Wheat probably would not have won the Democratic nomination. Wheat quickly solidified his hold on the district and easily dispatched primary opponents in later elections. Democrat Andrew Young carried a 60 percent white district in Atlanta in three elections before his appointment as ambassador to the United Nations.

Gary Franks, the first black Republican elected to the House since the Great Depression, has so far won three terms by less than impressive margins from an overwhelmingly white Republican district in northwestern Connecticut. Franks won only 52 percent of the vote in 1990, 44 percent in a three-way race in 1992, and 52 percent in 1994 even though his district routinely favors Republicans more than any other Connecticut district. Franks won the Republican nomination not in a primary, but at the GOP district convention.[11] Oklahoman J.C. Watts doubled black representation in the Republican Caucus in 1994. Thirteen of 5079 elections does not seem like enough evidence to support Swain's or Thernstrom's claims.

Liberal Democrats originally elected to the House while the district still had a white majority account for all but two of the nineteen elections won by whites in majority black districts. An African American invariably replaces them upon their retirement. Thomas Foglietta, redistricted into a narrowly majority black district for the 1992 elections, is currently the sole white representative from a black majority district.[12]

Republican Webb Franklin of Mississippi's Second District was the only white candidate to win an open seat in a majority black district. Franklin won the district in a very close, racially polarized contest in 1982. Though the district had a nominal black majority, whites composed a majority of the voting-age population and electorate. Franklin narrowly won reelection against the same black opponent in 1984 even though a federal court redrew the lines to assure that blacks composed a majority of the district's voting-age population prior to the election. African-American Mike Espy defeated Franklin in 1986. Espy easily won reelection four times by increasing margins thanks to his assiduous efforts to attract white support. The state legislature further increased the district's black population during the 1990 redistricting round and the seat seems likely to continue to elect an African American despite the replacement of Espy by the more confrontational Bennie Thompson.

Conducting a logistic regression of *black representative*, a dummy variable coded one for black representatives and zero otherwise, on several racial and nonracial district characteristics makes it possible in table 3.1 to accurately determine the relative influence of race compared to other demographic factors on the election of black representatives. The analysis includes nearly all elections since 1972. Two independent variables, *proportion black* and *proportion Latino*, measure the effect of a district's racial composition on the race of its representative.

Including nonracial control variables tests the impact of factors other than the racial composition of the district on the election of black representatives. *Median real family income* and *percent high school graduates* control for income and education. These measures should have negative coefficients if low-socioeconomic-status districts elect black representatives more often than high-socioeconomic-status districts. African Americans tend to represent urban areas with many foreign-born-residents and government workers. *Proportion urban, proportion foreign born*, and *proportion government workers* should have positive coefficients if these variables relate to the election of black representatives. Districts with large numbers of residents raised prior to the civil rights movement might provide lower levels of support for black candidates. *Proportion 65 and over* controls for the presence of large numbers of older residents in a district. *South*, a dummy variable coded one for districts in the South and zero otherwise, should have a negative coefficient if blacks find it harder to win election in the region because of unusually high levels of racial polarization and the historical strength of white supremacy. The breakdown of racial barriers may have made it easier for black candidates to win election over time. *Congress*, a variable sequentially numbering the elections, controls for temporal change in the ability of African Americans to win election to the House.

Column 1 of table 3.1 reports the results. The magnitude of the coefficient

TABLE 3.1

Logit Analysis of Black Representative
(Dependent Variable: Black Representative [Black = 1])

Variable	(1)	(2)	(3)
Intercept	−11.65	−14.68	−8.01
	(3.23)	(2.87)	(.36)
Proportion Black	24.95		16.52
	(1.95)		(.81)
Proportion Latino	9.11		3.96
	(2.41)		(.80)
Black District		6.87	
		(.47)	
Open Seat	.92	.89	
	(.36)	(.32)	
Median Real Family Income ($1000)	.06	−.07	
	(.04)	(.04)	
Proportion High School Graduates	12.76	4.95	
	(2.48)	(2.18)	
Proportion Urban	.18	6.29	
	(1.33)	(1.14)	
Proportion Resident in State for at Least	−7.22	.98	
Five Years	(3.18)	(2.56)	
Proportion Foreign-Born	−3.91	−4.77	
	(2.87)	(2.10)	
Proportion 65 and Over	12.31	7.91	
	(5.89)	(4.28)	
Proportion Government Workers	−12.45	9.53	
	(4.10)	(3.19)	
South (South = 1)	−1.34	−.18	
	(.40)	(.40)	
Congress (93rd = 0, 94th = 1, . . .	−.15	.03	
104th = 11)	(.08)	(.07)	
Number of Observations	4843	4843	4843
Log Likelihood	−199.18	−239.23	−261.38
Percent Predicted Correctly	98.39	98.72	98.02

Note: Black District = 1 only if four conditions are met: (1) Proportion Black + Proportion Latino > .5; (2) Proportion Black − Proportion Latino > −.15; (3) Proportion Black > .3; and (4) Proportion Latino < .5.

and the relatively small standard errors on proportion black and proportion Latino indicate that the racial composition of a district has a large and regularly predictable effect on the probability of a district electing a black representative to Congress. Running a logit of black representative on black district, a dummy variable controlling for the racial composition of the district, and the same set of demographic variables determines whether the

nonracial demographic variables influence the election of a black representative in even a small way. Black district equals one when the district meets
four separate conditions roughly corresponding to Grofman and Handley's
conditions for the election of a black candidate. First, blacks and Latinos
must collectively form a majority. Second, Latinos must not compose more
than one-half of the population since Latinos generally win Latino majority
districts. Third, the percent Latino cannot exceed the percent black by more
than 15 percent. African Americans usually win mixed majority-minority
districts even when Latinos slightly outnumber blacks because of relatively
low levels of participation by Latinos. Grofman and Handley suggest that
blacks win only mixed majority-minority districts in which blacks form a
plurality so this condition departs from their findings.[13] Finally, African
Americans must constitute at least 30 percent of the population since black
candidates need a black base.

Column 2 of table 3.1 presents the result of this logit analysis. The large
coefficient and tiny standard error on black district indicate that black districts have a much higher probability of electing black representatives. Most
of the coefficients and standard errors of the nonracial demographic variables changed dramatically between the first and second logits. This sharp
shift suggests the absence of strong stable relationships between nonracial
demographic characteristics and the race of the representative.[14]

Varying each of the demographic variables over their entire actual ranges
in past apportionments reveals the utter failure of nonracial characteristics
to explain the race of a district's representative. All seats are treated as open
and outside the South in order to maximize the probability of electing a
black representative from nonblack districts since the logit results imply
that open and non-Southern districts elect black representatives more often
than other districts. The more recent the election, the more likely that a
district selects a black representative, so all seats are treated as up for
election in 1994. None of the nonracial demographic variables has even a
negligible impact on the election of a black representative. The election of
an African American from a non-majority-minority district is an incredibly
unlikely event.

Threshold for Election: The 65 Percent Rule Is Wrong

In *Kirksey v. Board of Supervisors of Hinds County,* the Fifth Circuit Court
of Appeals ruled that the minority percentage of majority-minority districts
created under the Voting Rights Act must provide members of the minority
group a "realistic opportunity to elect officials of their choice." Rather than
mandating merely black majority districts, some argue for 65 percent black
districts to compensate for higher levels of voting-age population, registration, and turnout among whites compared to blacks. Others attack the 65

TABLE 3.2
Probability of a Black Representative

Percent Latino	Percent Black							
	25	30	35	40	45	50	55	60
0	< .01	< .01	.01	.08	.28	.60	.86	.97
10	< .01	< .01	.03	.16	.43	.74	.93	.99
20	< .01	.01	.08	.27	.59	.85	.97	> .99
30	< .01	.03	.15	.42	.73	.93	.99	> .99
40	.01	.07	.26	.57	.84	.97	> .99	> .99

Note: Probabilities presented in this table derive from the logit results in column 3 of table 3.1

percent threshold as unnecessarily arbitrary. The Voting Rights Section of the Justice Department has used the 65 percent rule to defend its denial of preclearance of redistricting plans under Section 5, but claims that it judges each case individually and does not attach "special significance" to the 65 percent threshold.[15]

Civil rights advocates strongly endorse the 65 percent rule, but Grofman and Handley's research indicates that raising the minority population above 50 percent should guarantee the election of a black representative. Carol Swain agrees that the 65 percent threshold is much too high and too rigid. She claims that near majority-minority districts will elect blacks and that even districts with a lower proportion of blacks may send African Americans to Congress.[16]

Conducting a logit of black representative on the two key variables, proportion black and proportion Latino, makes estimating the threshold for the election of black candidates a straightforward task. Column 3 of table 3.1 displays the result of the logit analysis and table 3.2 shows the probability of a district electing a black representative to Congress for various percentages of blacks and Latinos in the district. The probability of a district sending an African American to Congress rises dramatically between 45 and 55 percent for a district with no Latino residents. Districts with a bare majority of black residents have a 60 percent chance of electing a black to the House. Raising the black share of the district's population by a mere 5 percent increases the probability of electing a black to 86 percent—a 26 percent increase. Fifty-five percent black majority districts should allow African Americans to elect a black representative if they so choose in most areas of the country. Even if these narrowly black majority districts lack a black majority in the voting population, black candidates receive sufficient white votes to win election. Increasing the black percentage in a district much above 55 percent wastes black votes. "Packing" has long been a strategy used by whites wanting to minimize black influence over the political process.[17]

Districts with a 45 percent black population have a 28 percent chance of sending a black representative to Washington. Black candidates apparently can attract enough white liberal support to win election even without a black majority in some congressional districts. Districts below 45 percent black almost never elect black representatives. Most black candidates find the prospect of attracting enough white votes to form a winning biracial coalition too daunting a prospect, so they do not seek election to the House from solidly white majority districts. The few black candidates who make the attempt fail to win sufficient white support to carry the district.

Several factors can raise or lower the threshold for the election of a black representative: the percentage of Latinos, the level of racial polarization, and racial differences in voter registration and turnout rates. Table 3.2 indicates that the percentage of blacks needed to make likely the election of an African American declines as the percentage of Latinos rises. Increasing the percentage of Latinos by 5 percent does not raise the probability of an African American winning the seat by nearly as much as increasing the percentage of blacks by 5 percent but the presence of a sizable Latino population still has a noticeable impact. In a 45 percent black district, raising the percentage of Latinos from 0 to 10 percent increases the probability of electing an African American from 28 to 43 percent.

Variation in the level of racial polarization, and differences between whites and blacks in the rates of voter registration and turnout mean that instituting a blanket national percentage black for the creation of a black district would ignore crucial differences between individual states and regions. A nominally black majority district may actually have a white voting-age majority because fewer blacks are of voting age than whites. Socioeconomic disparities between blacks and whites can exacerbate this racial difference between percentage of the population and turnout. Past studies have found that education strongly relates to registration and turnout at the polls.[18] The black population has generally received less education than the white population, so blacks vote at a lower rate than whites. If intense racial polarization exists, whites can prevent the election of a black to office in some black majority districts.

The Second District of Mississippi with its history of extreme racial polarization and black poverty demonstrates this truth vividly. The district had a black majority, but a white voting-age majority in 1982, and the black candidate lost by a narrow margin. For the 1984 elections, the district boundaries were redrawn to have a 58 percent black majority. The same black candidate lost again despite a vigorous campaign and strong black support. African-American Mike Espy, who had a strong organization in the black community and made a strong effort to calm white fears, finally won the district by a narrow margin in 1986. Racial polarization can work to the benefit of blacks in black majority districts. The 1990 redistricting increased the Second District's black percentage to 63 percent. Racial polarization assured the election of Bennie Thompson, vigorously opposed by virtually the entire white population of the district, over a white candidate in a 1993 special election. The decline of racial polarization can make it possible for blacks to win election even in solidly white areas. A number of overwhelmingly white cities, such as Denver, Seattle, Dallas, and Los Angeles have elected black mayors in elections in which race was not highly salient. Local differences should be taken into account when determining the threshold at which a congressional district will probably elect a black representative.

Latino Representatives

Latinos Win in Latino Voting Majority Districts

The relationship between percent Latino in a congressional district and the election of a Latino representative parallels the link between percent black and victorious black candidacies. The probability of a non-Latino gaining election declines as the percentage of Latinos in a district rises. Whether Latinos form a majority in the district seems to be the key factor in determining if a Latino or non-Latino represents the district. Non-Latinos won 5161 of the 5190 elections in Latino minority districts. Latinos carried the day in 82 of the 105 elections in Latino majority districts.

Examining the few exceptions to the general pattern only serves to reinforce the importance of ethnicity. Ten of the twenty-three elections won by non-Latinos in Latino majority districts were won by four representatives in districts that lacked Latino majorities in the voting-age population. Five of the remaining thirteen elections occurred in two districts in which the Latino voting-age population did not exceed 55 percent of the population and the citizen voting-age population was probably even lower. From 1982 until his death in 1989, Claude Pepper easily won reelection from a Miami district after being redistricted into a district with a 50.3 percent Latino voting-age majority. Pepper's unswerving condemnation of Castro and support of Israel undoubtedly gained him support among the large Cuban and Jewish populations in his district. In 1992 and 1994, white Gene Green narrowly defeated his Latino opponent in the Democratic primaries for a newly drawn Latino majority district in Houston with a 55 percent Latino voting-age population. Extremely low levels of voter registration among district Latinos greatly hampered Green's Latino opponent in this low-turnout district. The great diversity among Houston's Latino population, which came to America from all over Central America as well as Mexico, contributed to infighting among Latino leaders that worked to Green's benefit.[19]

Texan Ron Coleman accounts for the remaining eight elections. Throughout the 1980s, Coleman won reelection from his El Paso district along the

Mexican border despite the 60 percent Latino majority (55 percent among voting-age residents) in 1982. Over the course of the 1980s, the percentage of Latinos in Coleman's district gradually increased to 68 percent. Coleman easily defeated a Latino primary opponent in a newly drawn 70 percent Latino district in 1992. Strong Latino support was essential to Coleman's narrow victory over a white opponent in the 1992 general election. Coleman lost the white vote, but managed to win by garnering 80 percent of Latino votes.[20] Coleman easily dispatched a Latino Republican in the general election in 1994. Coleman, who retired in 1996, was the only white to represent a district in which Latinos constitute a clear voting majority.

All but one of the Latinos who garnered election from Latino minority districts won in majority-minority districts in which Latinos constituted a heavy plurality of the voters. Democratic Congressmen Edward Roybal, Herman Badillo, Robert Garcia, Esteban Torres and Robert Menendez won a total of fourteen elections from majority-minority districts with a Latino population of at least 40 percent between 1972 and 1994.[21] Democrat Bill Richardson of New Mexico has won seven elections since 1982 from a district that is currently about 35 percent Latino, 25 percent American Indian, and 40 percent white. Eight-term Republican congressman Manuel Lujan originally won election from a 49 percent Latino constituency in New Mexico in 1968. Lujan won reelection seven times. Although Lujan attracted significant Latino support, as a Republican, he probably benefited when the Latino percentage of his district declined to 37 percent following the 1980 reapportionment.

Running a logit of Latino representative on proportion Latino and the other nonracial demographic variables in table 3.3 more accurately measures the relative importance of proportion Latino in the population versus other demographic factors. Latino representative is coded one for Latino representatives, and zero otherwise. Column 1 of table 3.3 presents the result of this logit analysis. The only factors that truly matter are proportion Latino and proportion resident in the state for at least five years. The latter variable effectively serves as a proxy for citizenship. A large percentage of the Latinos who have not resided in their current state of residence for more than five years moved to the United States only recently and have yet to acquire American citizenship. Lacking access to the ballot, the most basic of political resources, noncitizens usually find it difficult to influence the political process.

The proportion of Latinos and the proportion of citizens interact to predict the election of a Latino representative. Increasing the proportion of Latinos in a district provides a more amenable political environment for Latino candidates. However, if these Latinos are not citizens, Latino candidates cannot win their votes and the district may lack a Latino voting majority. The low turnout in many Latino majority districts reflects the large legal

TABLE 3.3

Logit Analysis of Latino Representative

(Dependent Variable: Latino Representative [Latino = 1])

Variable	(1)	(2)	(3)
Intercept	−12.67	−.82	−4.81
	(8.60)	(3.05)	(6.75)
Proportion Latino	−8.22		−8.22
	(18.73)		(16.61)
Proportion Black	.49		
	(2.51)		
Latino Majority District		−20.66	
		(6.48)	
Proportion Resident in State for at Least	2.18	−.22	−3.85
5 years	(9.08)	(2.90)	(7.87)
Proportion Latino × Proportion Resident in	32.85		29.09
State for at Least Five Years	(21.86)		(19.45)
Latino District × Proportion Resident in State		28.94	
for at Least Five Years		(7.63)	
Open Seat	.54	.13	
	(.50)	(.43)	
Mean Real Family Income ($1000)	.04	−.17	
	(.08)	(.04)	
Proportion High School Graduates	1.88	.16	
	(3.60)	(2.25)	
Proportion Urban	−2.54	.53	
	(2.25)	(.97)	
Proportion Foreign Born	.92	8.91	
	(2.82)	(1.76)	
Proportion 65 and Over	3.95	−22.83	
	(6.41)	(5.12)	
Proportion Government Workers in	12.90	12.45	
Labor Force	(6.69)	(3.26)	
Congress (93rd = 0, 94th = 1, . . .	−.17	−.07	
104th = 11)	(.10)	(.07)	
Number of Observations	4843	4843	4843
Log Likelihood	−121.75	−208.87	−134.59
Percent Predicted Correctly	99.11	98.80	99.03

immigrant and illegal alien population unable to register or to cast ballots in congressional elections. An astoundingly low 13 percent of the voting-age population voted in the contested 1992 congressional election in the 84 percent Latino Thirty-Third District of California.[22] Predominantly black or white districts in California had much higher turnouts. Although black turnout is lower than white turnout, the racial differential is rarely high enough to prevent the election of black representatives.[23] The probability of electing a Latino representative also increases as the proportion of long-term residents, and therefore citizens, rises.

Running a logistic regression of Latino representative on Latino district, proportion resident in the state for at least five years, an interaction between these two variables, and the same set of demographic variables as in the first logit reveals whether a Latino majority district is a necessary precondition for the election of a Latino representative to Congress. Latino district is coded one for Latino majority districts and zero otherwise. Column 2 of table 3.3 presents the result of the logit analysis. Varying any of the demographic variables while holding the other variables constant at their means fails to raise the probability of electing a Latino to even .01 for non-Latino majority districts. Non-Latino majority districts rarely elect Latinos to Congress.

Threshold for Election Depends on the Proportion of Citizens in the Population

Conducting a logit of Latino representative on proportion Latino, proportion resident in the state for at least five years, and an interaction of these two variables to more precisely determines the threshold at which Latinos gain election. Column 3 of table 3.3 displays the results. Table 3.4 shows how the probability of a district sending a Latino to Congress varies with the percentage of Latinos and the percentage of long-term residents. A Latino candidate actually has a higher probability of winning election to Congress than a black candidate for comparable percentages of Latinos and African Americans, respectively, if one assumes that all of a district's residents have lived in their state of residence for more than five years, and thus that a high proportion of Latino residents have American citizenship.[24] There is a 38 percent chance that a 40 percent Latino district will have a Latino representative, but a 40 percent black district has only an 8 percent chance of having a black representative. Latinos would find it easier to overcome the electoral barrier than African Americans if all Latinos were citizens.

Unfortunately for Latinos, as the proportion of long-term residents declines, the probability of a district having a Latino representative drops dramatically. When the proportion of long-term residents falls to 80 percent, the probability of a district sending a Latino to Congress drops below the probability of electing an African American for comparable proportions of Latinos and blacks. Eighty-five percent of the residents of the average congressional district have lived in their current state of residence for at least five years. Interestingly, at this level, the probability of a Latino representing a district for any given percentage of Latinos in the district corresponds to the probability of an African American representing a district with the same percentage of black constituents.[25] At 55 percent, the percentage of Latinos needed to assure the election of a Latino corresponds to the percentage of blacks needed to assure the victory of an African American. The prob-

TABLE 3.4
Probability of a Latino Representative

% State Residents 5+ Years	Percent Latino										
	35	40	45	50	55	60	65	70	75	80	85
60	< .01	< .01	< .01	< .01	.02	.06	.13	.26	.42	.60	.77
65	< .01	< .01	< .01	.02	.08	.18	.36	.57	.76	.89	.96
70	< .01	< .01	.02	.08	.20	.41	.65	.84	.95	.99	> .99
75	< .01	.01	.06	.18	.41	.68	.87	.97	.99	> .99	> .99
80	< .01	.03	.13	.36	.65	.87	.97	> .99	> .99	> .99	> .99
85	.01	.07	.26	.57	.84	.97	> .99	> .99	> .99	> .99	> .99
90	.02	.14	.42	.76	.95	.99	> .99	> .99	> .99	> .99	> .99
95	.05	.24	.61	.89	.99	> .99	> .99	> .99	> .99	> .99	> .99

Note: Probabilities presented in this table derive from the logit results in column 3 of table 3.3.

ability of a district sending an African American to Congress for any given percentage of blacks varies with the percentage of Latinos in the district. The probability of a Latino representing any district for any given percentage of Latinos similarly varies with the percentage of long-term residents or citizens in the district.

These results provide more long-term hope for the election of greater numbers of Latinos than African Americans. As the proportion of Latinos rises and as greater numbers of Latinos gain American citizenship, the number of Latinos elected to Congress should increase, particularly if the Voting Rights Act forces states to create more Latino majority districts. The increase in the African-American share of the population is much slower. Unlike Latinos, blacks cannot look forward to substantial gains based on increases in the level of black citizenship. Additional African Americans might win congressional seats through the creation of new majority-minority districts in which blacks constitute a plurality due to the increase in the number of Latinos. It seems more likely that the larger Latino population will desire to elect Latinos to Congress and either overwhelm the black population in some seats currently held by blacks or, more likely, simply press for the creation of new Latino majority districts.

Pressure for Minority Representation Facilitates the Election of New Black and Latino Representatives from Majority-Minority Districts

Once a majority-minority district has been created, a great deal of pressure is placed on white candidates to vacate the district in order to make way for a black or Latino candidate. Black and Latino politicians often call for whites to step aside in order to allow minority politicians to advance. White politicians join their minority colleagues in pressuring whites to abandon minority districts as a means of appeasing minority politicians and residents, keeping their part of political bargains surrounding redistricting, and out of fear that courts will invalidate redistricting plans if a majority-minority district elects a white to office.

Numerous examples of pressure by blacks, Latinos, and whites on whites to abandon minority districts abound. Jesse Jackson called for the election of Donald Payne over Peter Rodino in New Jersey solely on the basis of the difference in the color of the candidates skin.[26] Democrat Robin Tallon of South Carolina left Congress after being redistricted into a majority black district because his initial decision to seek reelection stirred up racial animosities that he had long worked to end. Alex McMillan of Maryland was attacked by whites and blacks for considering seeking reelection in a majority black district after his old district was cut to pieces as part of an effort to create a new majority black district while protecting another white incumbent. Luis Guttierez of Chicago found his path to Congress clear after white politicians, including Mayor Richard Daley, pressured potential white opponents to leave the district open for a Latino. Latinos do not cast a majority of the votes in this supposedly Latino majority district, so white withdrawal from the race clearly benefited Latino candidates generally, and Gutierrez specifically because he had Daley's support.[27]

These types of deals are not inherently bad. They form the lifeblood of politics and may promote increased ethnic harmony as ordinary African Americans and Latinos see members of their racial or ethnic groups advancing to higher office. These types of interracial political negotiations follow the pattern of interethnic political negotiations among European immigrant groups earlier in the century. During the 1990 redistricting round, the Voting Rights Act provided minority politicians a powerful tool to bring to redistricting debates with white politicians. Unless states adopted plans that provide for majority-minority districts, black and Latino politicians could sue for violations of the act. In some cases, the Justice Department beat them to the punch and declared the redistricting plan invalid because it lacked a sufficient number of black and Latino districts. At some point, the effort to divvy up America along racial and ethnic lines starts to look less like minorities getting their piece of the political pie and more like segregating America for political purposes. The Supreme Court's distaste for racial gerrymandering led it to declare in *Miller v. Johnson* that utilizing race as the "predominant factor" in drawing district lines is unconstitutional. Until whites demonstrate greater willingness to elect blacks and Latinos in more than just token numbers, creating majority-minority districts will nevertheless remain a central part of any strategy to assure that significant numbers of blacks and Latinos join their white colleagues in conducting the nation's business on Capitol Hill.

Conclusion

The number of majority-minority congressional districts has substantially increased over the past twenty-five years due to broad interpretation of the Voting Rights Act. The dramatic increase in African-American and Latino congressional representation in Congress has rested entirely on vastly improved access to the ballot combined with the creation of new majority-minority districts. Nonracial demographic variables, such as income and urbanicity, often exhibit a strong bivariate correlation with the race of a representative. The link between these variables and the election of a minority member of Congress rests entirely on the strong relation between the racial composition of the district and other demographic characteristics. African Americans and Latinos differ substantially from whites on a number of demographic measures, so black and Latino majority districts differ as well.

Majority-minority districts play a crucial role in the election of minority representatives, but the percentage of minority residents needed to assure the election of a minority member of Congress is lower than the 65 percent threshold articulated by some advocates of minority representation. Assuming a district has no Latino residents, a 50 percent black district has a 60 percent chance of electing an African American to the House. Raising the percentage of African Americans in the district to 55 percent increases the probability of the district having a black representative to 86 percent. The presence of Latinos lowers the threshold needed to assure the election of an African-American representative.

The average district with a bare Latino majority has a 57 percent chance of sending a Latino to Congress. Increasing the Latino percentage to 55 percent raises the probability of a Latino representative to 84 percent. Variation in the proportion of long-term residents, and therefore citizens, in the population has a major effect on the probability of a district electing a Latino to the House. As more Latinos become citizens and the Latino population continues to increase, more Latinos should gain election to the House. Even more significantly, the threshold for the election of Latinos should decline as the proportion of Latino citizens rises.

PART II

BLACK AND LATINO SUBSTANTIVE

REPRESENTATION

4

AFRICAN-AMERICAN AND

LATINO REPRESENTATION

THIS CHAPTER shifts the focus from the election of minority representatives to the representation of minority interests. African-American and Latino representation differs substantively from white representation in a number of ways. Black and Latino representatives and Latino representatives of different national origins often differ sharply on public policy. These differences reflect very real contrasts in both political preferences, history, and demographics of the people these members of Congress represent. Scrutinizing the political characteristics of representatives in the form of partisanship, seniority, and ideology elucidates variations in the preferences of minority representatives as well as disparities in the power of various groups of minority representatives to influence the policy process toward these goals.

Power at the Polls: Blacks and Latinos Overwhelmingly Win as Democrats and by Large Margins

Black, Latino, and white representatives differ substantially in terms of partisanship and margin of victory. Reflecting the overwhelming identification with the Democrats among African Americans, most black representatives caucus with the Democrats and win by intimidating margins. Latino representatives differ by national origin in their partisan leanings. Like African-American representatives, Puerto Rican representatives are invariably Democrats and win by huge margins in their heavily Democratic districts. Mexican Americans tend to vote for the Democrats, but Mexican-American support for the Democratic party is not nearly as unanimous as among blacks and Puerto Ricans. Elections are somewhat more competitive in Mexican-American districts and the occasional Republican carries these constituencies. Unlike Mexican Americans or Puerto Ricans, Cuban Americans usually support Republicans for election to the House.

Black Partisanship and Electoral Success

Black representatives have almost always been Democrats since African Americans began shifting from the Republicans to the Democrats during the New Deal era. Only three blacks have served as Republicans since Demo-

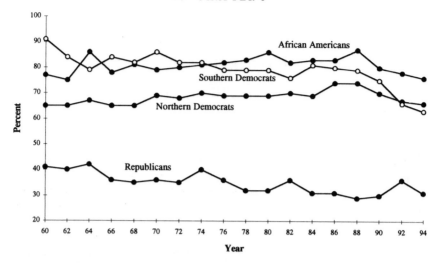

4.1. Average Democratic Vote by Race and Party. Democratic vote calculated as a percentage of the two-party vote. Unopposed representatives included as having received either 0 or 100 percent of the vote depending upon their party.

Sources: McGuiness, *American Leaders, 1789–1991*; *Guide to U.S. Elections* (Washington, D.C.: Congressional Quarterly, 1985): Duncan, *Politics in America*, various editions.

crat Arthur Mitchell defeated Republican Oscar DePriest for reelection in 1934. Unlike DePriest, none won election from a black majority district. Liberal Republican Edward Brooke won election to the Senate from Massachusetts in 1966 and 1972. Democrat Paul Tsongas defeated Brooke for reelection in 1978. Conservative Republican Gary Franks has represented an overwhelmingly white district in Connecticut since winning an open seat in 1990. Oklahoman J.C. Watts joined Franks in the House after winning election in 1994.

Election statistics reflect the strong Democratic partisanship of districts that elect black representatives. Black representatives consistently receive a higher share of the Democratic vote than the average Democrat. As figure 4.1 reveals, until the 1992 elections, southern Democrats regularly won by much greater margins than their northern Democratic and Republican colleagues. The average margin of victory for black representatives exceeded even that of southern Democrats, beginning with the 1976 elections. The average victorious Republican won by a margin of 38 percent and the average northern Democrat had a 33 percent margin of victory in 1994. Meanwhile, the average southern Democratic representative led by only 26 percent of the vote, but the mean African-American representative won by a thumping 53 percent. Figure 4.1 and these statistics were calculated including unopposed representatives as having received 100 percent of the vote. Excluding unopposed representatives lowers the proportion of the Democratic vote received by both Democratic and African-American representatives without changing the overall relationship between the two groups of representatives.[1]

The increasing competitiveness of southern congressional elections in the 1970s and 1980s relates directly to the shift in partisanship among blacks. The same racial liberalism that attracted blacks to the Democrats repelled racially conservative southern whites. Figure 4.1 shows that the trend towards competitive elections in the South has continued in the 1980s. As more and more southern whites abandoned the Democratic party, Democratic dominance of southern politics eroded and the electoral distinctiveness of southern Democrats vanished in the 1990s.[2] The mean southern Democrat actually won by a smaller margin than the average northern Democrat in the 1994 elections.

This unusually high Democratic vote in districts represented by blacks reflects that most African-American members of Congress come from black majority districts and African Americans are the most reliable group of Democratic partisans in America today. The percentage of blacks identifying with the Democratic party has regularly topped 75 percent in the National Election Study surveys since 1964. Identification with the Republicans among blacks has rarely exceeded 10 percent.[3] It is hardly accidental that black partisan leanings solidified around 1964. As Katherine Tate explains:

> The surge in black identification with the Democratic party in the 1964 election was largely the result of the new racial liberalism of the party, and more specifically, the enactment of civil rights legislation during the Kennedy-Johnson administrations. . . . In addition to the voting rights bill enacted in 1965, Kennedy's successor, Lyndon Johnson, would later sign into law a number of civil rights bills, including the 1964 Civil Rights Act, an omnibus bill that included a mandate for implementing school desegregation, and the 1968 Civil Rights Act. He would also initiate the War on Poverty, a set of federal programs aimed at creating new social service structures that would greatly benefit poor blacks.[4]

Just as the Democrats moved to identify themselves with racial liberalism, the Republicans shifted toward conservatism on racial issues. Edward G. Carmines and James A. Stimson rightly argue that Senator Barry Goldwater's outspoken stance against the Civil Rights Act of 1964 during his presidential campaign played a critical role in identifying the Republicans with racial conservatism.[5] African Americans quickly moved toward the Democrats, the party of racial liberalism, once race became a partisan issue.

Latino Partisanship and Electoral Success

Figure 4.2 reveals the wide variation in the average Democratic vote between national-origin subgroups of Latino representatives. Only one Puerto Rican and one Cuban-American representative served in any individual Congress prior to the 1992 elections, so interpreting the results for these

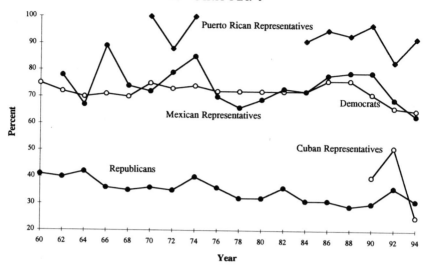

4.2. Average Democratic Vote by Latino Subgroups and Party. Democratic vote calculated as a percentage of the two-party vote. Unopposed representatives included as having received either 0 or 100 percent of the vote depending upon their party.

Sources: McGuiness, *American Leaders, 1789–1991*; *Guide to U.S. Elections*; Duncan, *Politics in America*, various editions.

subgroups requires caution. The extremely high proportion of the Democratic vote received by the Puerto Rican representative reflects the Democratic tendencies of the Puerto Rican district in the Bronx, New York, and compares to the proportion received by the Democrats in black districts in New York City. The two new Puerto Rican districts created in Chicago and Brooklyn during the 1990 redistricting cycle cast a similarly heavy Democratic vote. No Puerto Rican Republican has ever won a congressional seat. Seventy-one percent of the Puerto Rican respondents to the Latino National Political Survey reported that they favored the Democrats, while only 17 percent claimed to lean toward the Republicans.[6]

The average Democratic percentage in districts represented by Mexican Americans tracks the overall average Democratic vote, particularly during the second half of the period under study. Like Puerto Ricans, Mexican Americans tend to strongly support Democrats. Seventy-three percent of Mexican Americans reported voting for the Democratic candidate in the 1988 congressional elections, compared to 50 percent of whites.[7] Mexican-American support for the Democrats is not quite as unanimous or as predictable as black support in congressional elections. Though the vast majority of Mexican-American representatives serve in the House as Democrats, two Mexican Americans have caucused with House Republicans. Manual Lujan represented Albuquerque, New Mexico, in the House from 1969 to 1989. His district had a substantial, though not majority, Latino population. Republican Henry Bonilla resoundingly defeated incumbent Democrat Albert Bustamante in 1992 with 59 percent of the vote. Neither Bustamante's Mexican background nor Democratic partisanship helped him deflect charges of having lost touch with his constituents by bouncing checks at the House bank and buying a very expensive house in this very poor south Texas district. Bonilla easily won reelection in 1994.

Unlike Mexican Americans and Puerto Ricans, most Cuban Americans identify themselves as Republicans. Seventy-eight percent of Cuban Americans voted for the Republican candidate in the 1988 congressional elections, a far higher level of support for the Republicans than either Mexican Americans or Puerto Ricans gave the Democrats.[8] Cuban Americans are probably among the last anticommunist voters in America. Most Cuban immigrants fled the Castro regime in Cuba and identify with the Republicans as the party tougher on communism. Cuban-American concern about events in the home country parallels the political experience of many other ethnic groups in America. Just as African Americans took the lead in opposing apartheid in South Africa, and Jewish groups vocally support Israel, Cuban Americans pressure American leaders to undermine the Castro regime.

Two Republicans and one Democrat of Cuban ancestry currently serve in Congress. Both Republicans, Ileana Ros-Lehtinen and Lincoln Diaz-Balart, represent heavily Cuban-American districts in the Miami area. New Jersey Democrat Robert Menendez represents a 41 percent Latino district with a heterogenous Latino population. Menendez's partisanship reminds the observer of the political diversity within any ethnic group. Cuban Americans may generally take hawkish positions on foreign policy, but many support liberal policies on domestic programs. Most Cuban Americans may support the Republicans, but there are plenty of exceptions.

Power in the House: Seniority and Minority Influence

The increase in the number of minority members of Congress will seem a hollow achievement if African-American and Latino legislators cannot gain access to power within the House. Minorities support the election of minority officials in the hope of gaining greater responsiveness by government to their concerns. Seniority is not the only measure of congressional influence, but seniority matters a great deal because access to positions of power within the House relates directly to years of service. Junior members usually gain subcommittee and committee chairmanships by waiting for more senior members to retire or to die. The seniority system has been greatly undermined in recent years through the election of committee chairmanships and an increased ability to amend legislation on the House floor.[9] Speaker

Newt Gingrich further eroded the seniority system by installing his loyal lieutenants in place of more senior Republicans as committee chairs on some committees, including the important Appropriations Committee. Although the influence of junior members on legislation has risen, most members still gain additional staff and influence by ascending the rungs of power to the ranks of subcommittee and committee chairs. Italian-American Peter Rodino wielded tremendous influence over civil rights legislation on behalf of his African-American constituents as chairman of the House Judiciary Committee.

Studying seniority patterns helps determine whether minority representatives have attained similar positions of stature within the House. Ironically, while Southern Democrats in senior positions formerly used their influence to thwart civil rights legislation, African-American and Mexican-American legislators have risen to positions of real influence under the seniority system. Puerto Rican and Cuban-American representatives have found gaining access to power more difficult because of their small numbers.

The Pre–Voting Rights Act Era

Southern white committee chairmen used their power to kill civil rights measures supported both by the Democratic leadership and a majority of the chamber prior to the entrance of blacks on the southern political scene. Until the civil rights era and the resulting upsurge in partisan competition in the South, southern Democratic incumbents faced little competition for reelection, so they accrued much more seniority than their northern colleagues. As figure 4.3 shows, in 1963, southern Democrats had an average of four years more seniority than northern Democrats. Southern Democrats consequently chaired a disproportionate number of committees and had an outsized influence on legislation. Virginia Democrat Howard Smith, chairman of the House Rules Committee, bottled up civil rights bills by refusing to convene his committee for months on end. Smith was famous for abandoning the House for his Virginia farm, leaving the Rules Committee unable to conduct business.[10]

The willingness of chairmen like Smith to abuse their power made the fight to adopt civil rights legislation a decidedly uphill battle. Speaker Sam Rayburn fought successfully in 1961 to stack the Rules Committee with leadership loyalists to facilitate the passage of civil rights and other pressing legislation to the House floor. Unhappy with the continuing influence of conservative southern Democratic chairman, restive House liberals successfully pressed to open up the legislative process in the late-1960s and early 1970s.[11] The seniority gap between southern and northern Democrats vanished after the 1978 elections.

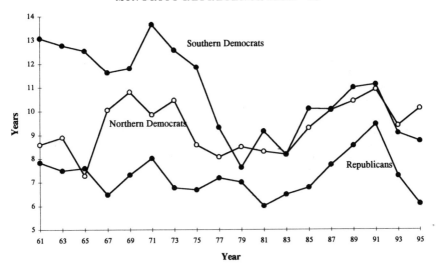

4.3. Average Seniority of Representatives by Party and Region.
Source: 1980 Census of Population and Housing, Summary Tape File 3A (Washington, D.C.: Bureau of the Census, 1982).

Black Seniority in the Post–Voting Rights Act Era

Comparing the seniority of black and Latino members of Congress to other members provides one measure of their influence within the House. Figure 4.4 plots the change in the average level of seniority for blacks, Democrats, and Republicans. The seniority of the average African-American representative plunged rapidly from twelve to four years between 1967 and 1971 due to the retirement of two senior members and the unprecedented election of a total of eight new black members in 1968 and 1970.[12] None of these new members left the House before 1978, so average black seniority steadily rose until it equaled the mean seniority level among all Democrats in 1977 despite the addition of four new black members in 1973 and one in 1975. Slow growth in the number of black representatives prevented serious deterioration in the average seniority of black members vis-à-vis the rest of the Democratic Caucus from 1977 through 1991. The normal pace of retirements and deaths prevented Black Caucus members from gaining greater average seniority than their peers.

Mean Republican seniority never rose above mean black seniority throughout this period. Seniority rankings only matter within parties because a senior Republican cannot take the place of a junior Democrat on a committee, so black Democrats did not benefit from their relatively high level of seniority compared to members of the opposition. African Americans benefited greatly from the seemingly endless Democratic control

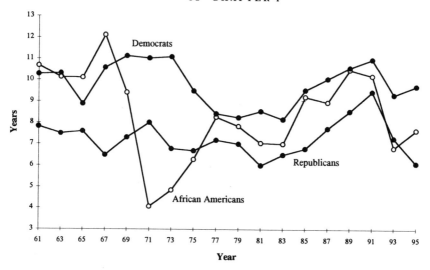

4.4. Average Seniority of Representatives by Race and Party.
Source: 1980 Census of Population and Housing, Summary Tape File 3A.

of the House. No Republican chaired a House committee between 1955 and 1994, but several blacks rose to positions of real power and influence with the House. William H. Gray III became majority whip, the third highest ranking position in the Democratic leadership, after serving as chairman of the Budget Committee from 1984 to 1988. African-American Democrats chaired three House committees until the Republicans won majority status in 1994. Dovish Ron Dellums presided over the Armed Services Committee, John Conyers chaired the Government Operations Committee, and William Clay wielded the gavel in the Post Office and Civil Service Committee. Blacks have been far more successful than another minority group within the House—women—at gaining influence. No woman has ever occupied one of the major leadership posts of either party. Under the Democrats in the 103rd Congress, no woman chaired a committee. Kansan Jan Meyers chaired the Small Business Committee in the Republican-controlled 104th Congress, but she retired in 1996. Neither of the African-American Republicans chaired a committee or subcommittee in the 104th Congress, though Gary Franks served as chairman of the Republican task force on welfare reform.[13]

The gap between average black and average Democratic seniority levels widened to 2.5 years in 1993 because of the election of thirteen new black members from new majority black districts and the defeat of two black incumbents in primaries in Chicago by other black candidates. Mean black seniority may soon rise above average Democratic seniority in future Congresses. African Americans retire at a lower rate and win reelection at a

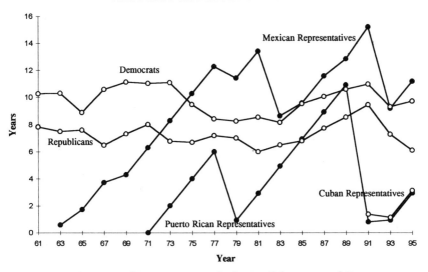

4.5. Average Seniority of Representatives by Latino Subgroups and Party.
Source: 1980 Census of Population and Housing, Summary Tape File 3A.

higher rate than other members.[14] The relative difficulty in winning higher office for blacks compared to whites discourages many black candidates from joining their white colleagues in seeking election as governor or to the Senate. A future seniority-lowering infusion of new black members seems unlikely since blacks represent all but one of the black majority districts.

The retirement of certain incumbent white representatives upon the creation of new majority-minority districts temporarily reduced black power within the House. The rise of so many new African-American legislators has mitigated the negative effect of this loss. The tendency for black members of Congress to pursue long congressional careers will probably result in a higher level of influence due to seniority over the long run.

Latino Seniority in the Post–Voting Rights Act Era

Figure 4.5 reveals in graphic detail the seniority problem facing groups represented by only one or a few members in the House. The Puerto Rican case exemplifies this problem perfectly. Herman Badillo continuously gained seniority after entering the House in 1971. All of this seniority was lost when he left the House in 1977 to become a deputy to New York City Mayor Edward Koch. Robert Garcia, Badillo's successor, gained even more seniority during his service from 1978 to 1990, but it was all lost when he resigned after his conviction. The three Puerto Ricans currently serving in the House possess very little seniority, but the increase in numbers expands the influence of the Puerto Rican community and limits the impact of losing

any one member. The situation of Cuban Americans in Congress today resembles that of Puerto Ricans. Both groups suffer from the small numbers
problem and need to work with other members to wield real clout. No
Puerto Rican or Cuban-American member chaired even a House subcommittee under the Democrats in the 103rd Congress. Cuban-American Ileana
Ros-Lehtinen chaired a House subcommittee—the Subcommittee on Africa
of the International Relations Committee—in the Republican dominated
104th Congress.

Puerto Rican and Cuban-American members have yet to benefit from the
seniority system, but two Mexican-American representatives from south
Texas chaired two important congressional committees until the Democrats
lost control of the House in 1994. Kika de la Garza chaired the Agriculture
Committee and Henry Gonzalez headed the Banking, Finance, and Urban
Affairs Committee. Their long service in the House made their ascension to
these high posts unsurprising. In 1995, de la Garza began his sixteenth term
and Gonzalez his seventeenth term. Average Mexican-American seniority
exceeded mean Democratic seniority from 1975 through 1994, often by
substantial amounts. The infusion of several new members in 1983 temporarily lowered mean Mexican-American seniority to normal Democratic
levels. All of the new members gained reelection throughout the 1980s and
Mexican-American seniority rapidly rose above average levels again. The
average Mexican-American representative had nearly three more years of
seniority than the average Democrat in 1991. This seniority combined with
their relatively high numbers make Mexican-American representatives a
much more formidable force in the House than their Cuban-American and
Puerto Rican colleagues. No Mexican-American representatives chaired
even a subcommittee under the Republicans in the 104th Congress. Henry
Bonilla, the sole Mexican-American Republican, sits on the prestigious
Appropriations Commitee, but lacks enough seniority to claim a subcommittee chairmanship.

Exercising their Power: Liberals, but Not Always

Minority activists press for the creation of majority-minority districts not just
for symbolic reasons but because they believe that black and Latino members of Congress will act differently than white representatives. This section
examines the extent to which black and Latino representatives vote differently than their white peers on the House floor as a prelude to the systematic
analysis in the next chapter of whether minority representatives vote differently than non-Latino white representatives after controlling for other factors. Before turning to the results, I discuss the primary measure of ideology
used throughout this work.

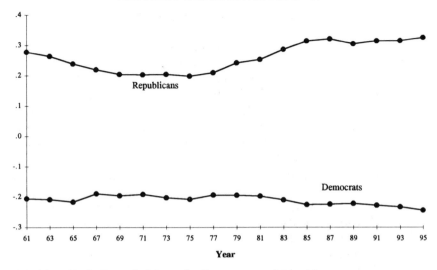

4.6. Mean Poole-Rosenthal Score for Democrats and Republicans.

Measuring Ideology: The Poole-Rosenthal Scores

In their spatial model of the roll-call voting behavior of U.S. representatives
(see figure 4.6), Keith Poole and Howard Rosenthal assigned two scores, or
dimensions, to every member of the House for each Congress. Each score
measures one orthogonal dimension of a member's voting behavior on the
floor of the House. Poole and Rosenthal estimated the scores using every re-
corded roll-call vote, except those with fewer than 2.5 percent of those voting siding with the minority. The estimation for each Congress excludes
members who cast less than twenty-five votes. Poole and Rosenthal found
that the first score correctly predicts 80 percent of roll-call voting decisions,
and the second score boosts the model's predictive power to 83 percent.
Adding more dimensions to the model fails to improve it.[15]

Poole and Rosenthal unsurprisingly found partisanship highly salient in
predicting roll-call votes because of the enduring nature of two-party politics in America. The first dimension corresponds to a scale measuring party
loyalty.[16] The more loyal the Republican, the higher the score. Conversely,
the more loyal the Democrat, the lower the score. The first dimension
ranged from −.851 to .778 between 1971 and 1985 with a mean score of
−.042 and a standard deviation around the mean of .30. The first dimension
captures much of the ideological division within the House of Representatives because of the relative liberalism of most Democrats compared to Republicans. During stable periods, including the period studied here, one dimension explains most roll-call voting behavior and a second dimension
adds little to the explanatory power of the model. A second dimension boosts

the explanatory power of the model when the party system is under stress by capturing divisions within the parties.[17]

Interest-group ratings serve as alternative measures of congressional ideology. Numerous groups, including Americans for Democratic Action (ADA), the Chamber of Commerce of the United States (CCUS), the AFL-CIO's Committee on Political Education (COPE), the American Conservative Union (ACU) and the National Abortion Rights Action League (NARAL), publish ratings of members of Congress based upon a number of "key votes" cast by the member over the course of a congressional session. These ratings range from 0 to 100 and reflect the percentage of key votes in which the representative's vote agreed with the interest group's position on that issue.

Interest-group ratings do not measure ideology as well as the Poole-Rosenthal scores. The Poole-Rosenthal scores not only better predict roll-call voting behavior in the U.S. House than interest group ratings, they are the best existing predictor of roll-call voting decisions. The Poole-Rosenthal scores reflect the total voting record of members of Congress, while interest-group ratings take only perhaps the most extreme votes into account. Interest-group ratings consequently contain much less information than the Poole-Rosenthal scores and do a poorer job of differentiating between members—the fundamental purpose of any scale. Ratings rarely take on even one-half of the potential integer values since they are based on only ten to fifteen actual roll-call votes. Many members receive the extreme possible scores of 0 or 100 from various interest groups. Unlike interest-group ratings, which take on only a few discrete values, the Poole-Rosenthal scores are continuously distributed.

Although this chapter uses only the Poole-Rosenthal scores to compare average ideology of various groups of members, the analysis of the relationship between race and ideology in the next chapter utilizes both the Poole-Rosenthal scores and interest-group ratings in order to make sure that the results do not depend upon using one type of measure or the other.

Partisan and Regional Differences

Critics of the American two-party system often complain that no significant ideological differences separate the two parties. Poole and Rosenthal found that party remains the most enduring cleavage within American politics. Figure 4.6 shows that the average Democrat and the average Republican vote quite differently on the floor of the House. Far from being like Tweedledee and Tweedledum, Democrats and Republicans tend to stake out opposing viewpoints on issues within the chamber. Party serves as a constraint on the votes of individual U.S. Representatives even though the U.S. Congress lacks the party discipline of the House of Commons in Britain or

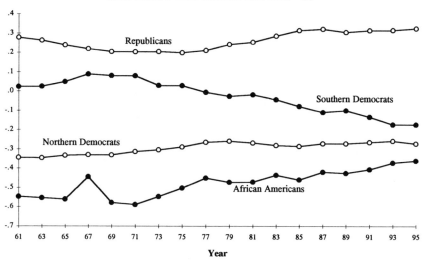

4.7. Mean Poole-Rosenthal Scores by Race, Party, and Region.

Canada. Knowing the party label of a representative allows one to predict with a great deal of probability, if not certitude, a representative's position on a particular issue.

Regional differences within the Democratic party have nevertheless persisted. Southern Democrats have voted much more conservatively than their northern party colleagues. The mean southern Democrat was actually closer to the mean Republican than the mean northern Democrat on the first Poole-Rosenthal score for the first half of the period under study. Southern Democrats benefited from their middle position between the Republican and northern Democratic blocs. Their votes were often essential to the passage of legislation. Southern Democratic apostasy hit its height between 1967 and 1971. Southern Democrats now vote much more like their northern colleagues, but still tend to be among the first to defect from the Democrats.

The Ideology of African-American Representatives

Figure 4.7 shows that black representatives have consistently been more liberal than Republicans and Democrats of both regions as measured by the first Poole-Rosenthal score. Discovering that African-American representatives invariably occupy the left end of the political spectrum in the House is hardly a shock. African-American representatives have consistently been among the most ardent congressional supporters of liberal policies. Black representatives staunchly supported the multiplication of social welfare programs during Lyndon Johnson's Great Society and opposed the rollback of these same programs as part of Reaganomics.

The position of black representatives on the left wing of the House may limit their influence. Liberal legislation often requires and receives black support in order to pass. Conservatives usually do not work to make their bills more appealing to blacks because African-American representatives generally will not support conservative legislation. As a centrist group, southern Democrats are often vital to the passage of legislation, so both conservatives and liberals often must modify bills to appease them in order to avoid defeat on the floor of the House.

Black representatives can attempt to use their influence to maintain the liberal character of legislation. The Congressional Black Caucus may risk the unpalatable final result of having no bill pass the House at all if it uses its clout to oppose changes to liberal bills. The Black Caucus's attempt to exert its influence in the fight over the 1994 crime bill vividly demonstrated the perils of opposing compromise bills. Several black members of Congress combined with Republicans to derail passage of the crime bill staunchly supported by President Clinton because the bill did not include provisions banning discriminatory implementation of the death penalty. Clinton made a few small concessions to black members in revising the bill, but the President also cut spending on preventive crime measures favored by African-American legislators as a concession to conservatives. The final bill did not include the death penalty provision because it would have made the bill unacceptable to a majority of the House. Black representatives can derail compromise bills supported by Democratic presidents with relative ease but they find it more difficult to draft new bills more to their liking that can still pass the House.

The Ideology of Latino Representatives

Figure 4.8 contrasts the mean Poole-Rosenthal scores for Latinos with Republicans as well as with northern and southern Democrats. The ideological position of Mexican-American representatives between northern and southern Democrats places them in the mainstream of the Democratic party. Mexican-American representatives have been more likely to support liberal legislation than southern Democrats. Through his roll-call voting behavior, the one Puerto Rican representative consistently aligned himself with African-American representatives on the liberal wing of both the House and the Democratic Caucus. The Poole-Rosenthal scores and interest-group ratings indicate that the one Cuban-American Democrat, Robert Menendez, has a solidly liberal voting record. The two Cuban-American Republicans from Florida vote substantially more conservatively than other Latinos but cast more liberal votes, particularly on labor issues, than white Republicans from their state. Treating Latinos as a unitary group would mask the diverse political behavior of Latinos of different national origins.

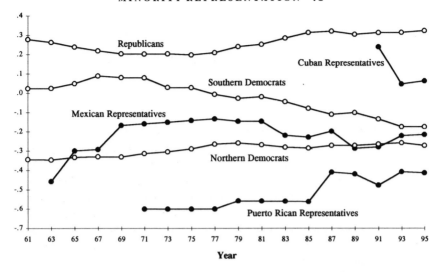

4.8. Mean Poole-Rosenthal Scores by Latino Subgroup, Party, and Region.

Conclusion

African-American and Puerto Rican legislators cast more liberal votes than the average member of the Democratic Caucus, but Mexican-American representatives fall within the center of the Democratic party. The average level of liberalism among African-American and Latino representatives matches closely the level of Democratic support among each of these groups. The seniority system has allowed black and Mexican-American legislators to gain access to some of the higher rungs of power in the House in the form of powerful committee chairs. Most minority representatives gained additional influence through long-term Democratic control of the House. Blacks and Latinos gained new access through the election of new African-American and Latino representatives despite the loss of some senior white representatives upon the creation of new majority-minority districts. The Democratic debacle in 1994 had a catastrophic effect on the number of minority committee chairs. No African-American or Latino representatives chaired a full committee and only one minority representative chaired even a subcommittee in the Republican controlled 104th Congress. Small numbers and low levels of seniority further limit access to power by Puerto Rican and Cuban-American representatives.

5

RACE AND REPRESENTATION

CHAPTER 3 demonstrated that the election of blacks and Latinos to the House of Representatives depends heavily upon the existence of majority-minority congressional districts. Majority-minority districts, however, may advance descriptive representation of blacks and Latinos without advancing substantive representation of minority interests. Representatives from majority-minority districts conceivably do not respond to African-American concerns more than representatives from black minority districts. More plausibly, creating majority-minority districts may make *individual* representatives more responsive to blacks and Latinos, but reduce the *aggregate* responsiveness of the House of Representatives to minorities.

Some researchers predict exactly this negative outcome to racial redistricting. Abigail Thernstrom claims that concentrating minorities in majority-minority districts heightens the responsiveness of one representative at the cost of losing influence over the representatives from surrounding districts. White representatives may not support minority interests after losing most of their minority constituents. Gaining one solidly supportive minority representative matters little if the white majority consistently outvotes that representative.[1] Opponents of this position, such as Frank Parker, argue that without minority representation, minority views will not gain any voice.[2]

This chapter explores the relation between the racial composition of a district and the ideology of its member of the House. Responsiveness to African-American interests abruptly jumps once a district reaches 40 percent black. Interestingly, this threshold for responsivenesss occurs at a much lower level than the 50 to 55 percent threshold generally required for the election of African-American representatives. Racial differences in registration and turnout rates may slightly raise or lower the threshold for heightened responsiveness.

Southern Democratic responsiveness to African Americans further increases linearly with the percentage of blacks above and below the 40 percent black threshold. Republicans, who rarely represent districts greater than 40 percent black, also support black interests more often as the percentage of blacks increases. Northern Democrats, however, show little change in ideology except when a district crosses the 40 percent black mark. Regional differences in the dispersion of blacks and the ideology of whites explain these differences. Racial redistricting tends to make surrounding districts more conservative and likely to elect Republicans in the South, but not the North. Racial redistricting increases black descriptive representation at the expense of black substantive representation in the South.

The chapter considers means of measuring responsiveness to African Americans before turning to the statistical analysis and discussion of redistricting. African Americans consistently hold substantially more liberal views on economic and racial issues than other Americans, so representatives cast more liberal roll-call votes when acting in accordance with the wishes of their black constituents. The chapter then moves to a description of the statistical model of race and ideology and then an analysis of the implications of the model for redistricting.

African-American Public Opinion

Measuring responsiveness to minority interests is a tricky endeavor. Individual members of any large group invariably have a variety of opinions on a number of issues. Black public opinion nevertheless is often quite cohesive and substantially more liberal than white opinion.

Economic and Social Welfare Policy

The General Social Survey has repeatedly uncovered large racial gaps in attitudes towards social welfare liberalism. African Americans consistently place responsibility for aiding the poor on the shoulders of government (see fig. 5.1). Only around one-quarter of whites hold similar views. Even after controlling for income, blacks support social welfare spending at a higher rate than whites.[3]

The racial gap persists upon examination of more specific social welfare policy areas. African Americans favor higher welfare spending far more frequently than whites (see fig. 5.2). Seventy-five to 90 percent of whites consistently oppose increases in welfare spending. White opposition to welfare reached its apogee during the Carter administration and moderated slightly after President Reagan slashed welfare spending. The percentage of blacks stating that the government spends too much on welfare has never exceeded one-third, and majorities of blacks have frequently favored increasing welfare spending.

Blacks and whites similarly disagree about the necessity for greater government spending on the problems of major cities. Large majorities of African Americans believe that the government does not allocate enough money to solving the problems of big cities (see fig. 5.3). Many whites think that government spends too little on the cities but fewer whites than blacks hold this view. The racial gap on this issue never closed completely for even a short period or shown signs of narrowing permanently despite varying between 12 and 28 percent over the past twenty-five years.

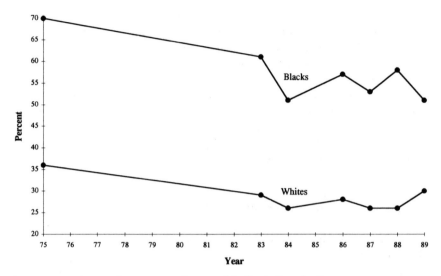

5.1. Percent Saying Government Responsible for Aiding the Poor.
Source: General Social Surveys, National Opinion Research Center; see Floris W. Wood, *An American Profile—Opinions and Behavior, 1972–1989* (Detroit: Gale Research, 1990).

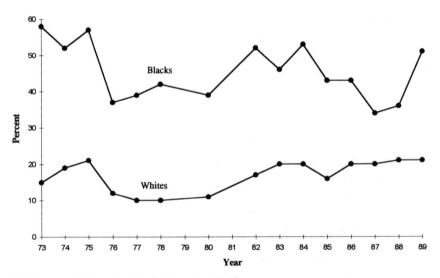

5.2. Percent Saying Too Little Spent on Welfare.
Source: General Social Surveys, National Opinion Research Center; see Wood, *An American Profile*.

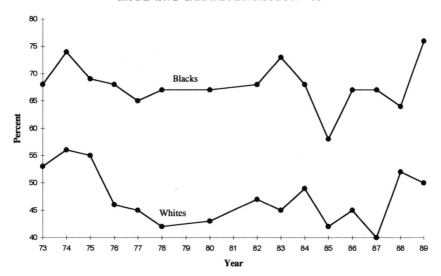

5.3. Percent Saying Too Little Spent on Big-City Problems.
   Source: General Social Surveys, National Opinion Research Center; see Wood, *An American Profile*.

   The relative socioeconomic statuses of the black and white communities make the persistence of a racial gap on social welfare issues far from surprising. Median white family income exceeded black median family income by $15,492 in 1990.[4] Thirty-two percent of African-Americans lived in poverty in 1990, a status shared by only 9 percent of white Americans. The ratio of black unemployment to white unemployment grew throughout the 1980s, increasing from 2.1 in 1981 to 2.8 in 1990. Relative economic depravation means that African Americans benefit disproportionately from social welfare spending, so it is no wonder that blacks favor it at a higher rate than whites. The relatively high concentrations of blacks in urban ghettos with high crime rates, poor health care, few job opportunities, and abysmal educational systems spur African Americans to support greater spending than whites on the problems of big cities. The roll-call voting behavior of representatives influenced by their African-American constituents reflects this racial gap. A representative's support for government spending on social welfare ills rises and black influence increases.

Racial Issues

Black and white Americans disagree substantially on the extent of progress that has been made on civil rights issues. The percentage of whites thinking that the situation of African Americans has improved rose steadily from 39 percent in 1964 to 65 percent in 1976. The percentage of blacks viewing

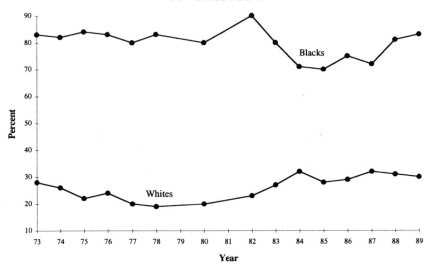

5.4. Percent Saying Too Little Spent on Blacks.
Source: General Social Surveys, National Opinion Research Center; see Wood, *An American Profile*.

their position as improved has declined from 60 percent in 1964 to 34 percent in 1976. Blacks and whites have strikingly different views about the pace of social change. Forty-five percent of blacks characterized the rate of civil rights progress as "too slow" in 1980 in contrast to under 10 percent of whites.[5] Racial differences in support for government intervention to improve the condition of blacks reflect this gap in beliefs about racial progress. Over 70 percent of blacks have consistently favored higher government expenditures to improve conditions for blacks since 1973 (see fig. 5.4). Only one-fifth to one-third of the whites supported similar new government outlays over the same time period.

Political Impact of the Racial Gap

Patterns of party identification and support for a party's presidential candidates follow these racial differences in attitudes towards social welfare and racial issues. African Americans overwhelmingly favor the Democrats, the party of economic and racial liberalism, over the more conservative Republicans. Seventy-three percent of African Americans said that they believe that the Democratic party works "very hard" or "fairly hard" on "issues Black people care about" when polled in 1984. The same percentage of African Americans thought that the Republicans worked "not too hard" or "not hard at all."[6] Over 80 percent of African Americans identify themselves as Democrats, while under 15 percent identify themselves as Republicans.[7]

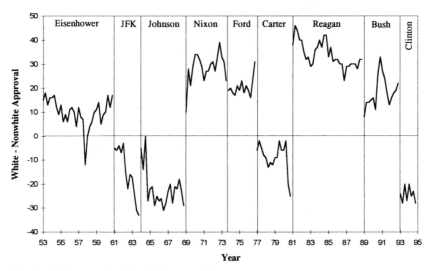

5.5. Racial Gap in Presidential Approval.
Source: Lyn Ragsdale, *Vital Statistics on the Presidency* (Washington, D.C.: Congressional Quarterly, 1996), Table 5-6.

Whites consistently approved of the performance in office of Republican Presidents Reagan and Bush at a higher rate than blacks according to Gallup surveys. President Ronald Reagan's staunch opposition to traditional social welfare programs and conservatism on racial issues marked his administration and inspired sharply different reactions among blacks and whites. The racial gap in presidential approval, generally quite narrow during the Carter administration, widened enormously upon Ronald Reagan's inauguration as president. Throughout most of Reagan's presidency, the percentage of whites approving of his handling of his job as president remained more than 30 percent higher than the percentage of blacks (see fig. 5.5). The racial gap in presidential approval declined when George Bush assumed the presidency, but gradually rose over the course of Bush's four years in office. In contrast, at least 20 percent more blacks than whites approved of Clinton's handling of his job as president during his first three years in office.

The racial gap in voting for president has existed even longer than the racial gap in presidential approval. African Americans have overwhelmingly supported Democratic presidential nominees for three decades, but a majority of whites have not voted for a Democratic president since Lyndon Johnson's landslide victory in 1964. Except for Jimmy Carter in 1976, no Democratic presidential nominee won more than 40 percent of the white vote over the same period. Over 80 percent of blacks voted for the Democratic nominee in each post-1964 presidential election. Racial polarization in presidential voting reached its height with the reelection of Ronald Reagan in 1984. Sixty-four percent of whites voted to reelect Reagan, but only 9 percent of blacks supported his reelection.[8]

The disproportionate negative effect of Reagan's tax and economic policies on blacks explains the intensity of black opposition to his reelection. Whites gained and blacks lost financially from the Reagan administration's policy of lowering taxes on the rich and raising taxes on the poor. People in the top quintile of income paid an average of $2,513 less in taxes while people in the bottom quintile paid an average of $137 more due to changes in the tax code between 1980 and 1985. Whites were far more likely to benefit from these changes than blacks. For every African American in the top quartile who paid less in taxes, 2.5 African Americans in the bottom quartile owed the government more money. The relationship was reversed among whites; 1.8 whites in the top quartile received a tax cut for every white who paid more tax. Minorities suffered disproportionately from cuts in programs such as AFDC (Aid to Families with Dependent Children) and food stamps.[9] Reagan's failure to press for strong implementation of civil rights laws or to appoint many black officials further alienated African Americans.

Modeling Responsiveness to African Americans

The substantial policy differences between blacks on whites on public policy suggest that varying the racial composition of a congressional district's population may affect the legislative behavior of the district's representative on the floor of the House of Representatives. The remainder of this chapter explores this question and the next chapter expands upon it by studying the aggregate effect of racial redistricting on public policy. Before turning to the results and the implications of the analysis, this section details the functional form and specification of the model of race and ideology as well as tests done to assure the accuracy of the model. Readers not interested in this technical discussion can skip ahead to the discussion of the implications of the results.

Model Specification

The statistical model used here is similar to that of linear regression analysis, but with an important twist in the estimation of the variance. The model permits the variance to shrink as the percentage of blacks rise, so it is not homoscedastic like linear regression models. The systematic component of the model is identical to the systematic component of a linear regression model. Let y be the dependent variable. Denote X as a vector of explanatory variables where the first element is a constant term. Let B be a vector of parameters. In both models, $E(y) = XB$. The stochastic component of the two models differs. The linear regression model assumes that the stochastic component is normally distributed with a mean of zero and a constant variance σ^2. The model employed here relaxes the homoscedasticity constraint of linear regression. Instead, σ^2 varies as a function of a set of explanatory variables so that $\sigma^2 = \exp(DK)$. D is a vector of explanatory variables where the first is a constant of all ones. K is a vector of parameters.[10] Maximum likelihood estimation was used to estimate the coefficients of the independent variables.

DEPENDENT VARIABLE

The Poole-Rosénthal scores measures the ideology of members of Congress and serves as the dependent variable. As explained more fully in chapter 4, the Poole-Rosenthal scores are the best existing predictor of congressional roll-call voting behavior. The higher the score, the more conservative the member of Congress. Martin Olav Sabo received the lowest and most liberal score of −.851 in 1985 over the course of the period studied here (1972–1990). Phil Crane earned the highest and most conservative score of .786 in 1989.[11] Interest group ratings correlate well with the Poole-Rosenthal scores. Models utilizing interest group ratings from ADA, COPE, and the LCCR produce virtually identical results to the model utilizing the Poole-Rosenthal scores.

EXPLANATORY VARIABLES

Three terms measure the impact of race on ideology: *proportion black, 40% black district,* and *proportion black × 40% black district.* These terms model a linear relationship between percentage black and ideology with a slope and intercept shift at 40 percent black. The previous chapter showed that blacks usually gain the ability to elect an African American to Congress upon becoming a majority of the district's population. The model with slope and intercept shifts at 40 percent black nevertheless empirically fits the data better than a model with a slope and intercept shift at 50 percent black as well as many other alternative specifications tested in the process of developing the model.[12] This model plausibly represents how the electoral system and racial bloc voting mold the relationship between race and ideology despite its empirical derivation. The results section will discuss the implications of this model for race and representation.

Democrat, a dummy variable, measures partisan differences in ideology. Race influences the party as well the ideology of a representative. Controlling for party as well as race makes it possible to assess the effect of racial compared to partisan redistricting. Mapmakers can draw Democratic as well as black majority districts during redistricting. Evaluating the overall effect of pursuing either of these goals is impossible without knowing the contrasting effects of creating a new black majority or Democratic district on ideology.

Party interacts with several of the other demographic variables, so interaction terms, discussed below, control for these effects as needed. Measuring the total impact of party compared to race requires taking the coefficients on all of these terms into account. Statistical trials run on separate models for Democrats and Republicans tested for interactions between party and other variables. Interaction terms between party and a variable were added when the variable had different effects on the ideology of representatives of different parties. The model excludes variables that had no visible effect on either ideology or the coefficients of the other variables.

Many districts with large numbers of African Americans also contain large numbers of Latinos. Controlling for the presence of Latinos prevents confounding the effect of proportion black with proportion Latino. *Proportion Latino* and *proportion Latino × Democrat* serve this purpose. The interaction term controls for the different effect of the presence of Latinos in Democratic and Republican districts. Increasing the proportion of Latinos makes Democratic representatives more liberal, but spurs Republican representatives to vote more conservatively. The diversity of public opinion among Latinos probably accounts for the difference. Puerto Ricans generally hold liberal opinions and vote heavily Democratic. Mexican Americans as a group are more moderate and a sizable minority vote Republican. Cuban Americans support conservative policies more often than either Puerto Ricans or Mexican Americans and a majority of Cuban Americans regularly cast Republican ballots.[13]

South and *south × Democrat*, control for the relative conservatism of southern members of Congress. Southern representatives in both parties cast more conservative roll-call votes than their northern peers. The positive coefficient on the interaction term reflects greater regional differences in legislative behavior among Democrats compared to Republicans. The high degree of conservatism among northern Republicans compared to the liberalism of northern Democrats makes it easier for southern Democrats to move to the right of their party colleagues.

Urban districts elect relatively liberal members of Congress even after controlling for race, party, and region. Residents of urban areas may elect relatively liberal delegations because they benefit more from liberal economic programs. High concentrations of white ethnic voters with historical ties to the Democrats may further explain the liberalism of urban representatives. *Proportion urban* captures the relative liberalism of urban versus rural representatives. The inclusion of this variable assures that the coefficients on the racial variables reflect the impact of the presence of blacks, rather than their location in an urban area.

Proportion 65 and over controls for the propensity of districts with a high proportion of elderly residents to elect relatively liberal representatives. The generational shift in party identification from Demcratic to Republican probably explains this pattern. Older Americans may fondly recall liberal New Deal programs and depend on government programs like Social Security and Medicaid, but younger Americans often remember the conservatism of the Reagan and Bush years and view government as a burden. Elderly Americans vote in large numbers, so representatives ignore them at their peril. Even conservative representatives from districts in places like Florida with large numbers of elderly residents vocally support social welfare programs like Social Security and Medicare.

Republican representatives become more conservative as the level of education rises. *Proportion high school graduates × Republican* controls for this effect. Empirical tests revealed no relationship between education and ideology in Democratic districts. Excluding the term measuring the effect of education on Democratic ideology does not change the coefficients of the racial variables, so the model omits it. Income has only a marginal effect on the ideology of a representative after controlling for education. Perhaps surprisingly, members cast more liberal votes on the House floor as the *deflated median family income* of a district rises.

First year elected × Republican controls for the effect of seniority on Republican ideology. New Republican members of Congress vote more conservatively than their more senior peers. This generational shift mirrors the changing makeup of the Republican Caucus. Exceedingly conservative southerners, like Newt Gingrich, have risen in prominence as liberal northerners, like Jacob Javits, have dwindled. Empirical analysis uncovered no relationship between seniority and ideology among Democrats.

Margin of victory × Democrat completes the list of explanatory terms in the model of ideology. Democrats who won by a large margin cast more conservative roll-call votes than other Democrats. This specification supports the conclusions of scholars who think that moderates win by greater margins than party ideologues.[14] Empirical analysis did not reveal any relationship between margin of victory and liberalism among Republicans.

The variance term of the model, σ^2, depends on only one variable: proportion black. The variance declines as the proportion of blacks in the population rises. This result makes sense because African-American public opinion is relatively cohesive compared to white opinion. Race should become more salient and have a more deterministic effect on ideology as the proportion of black rises. After all, race should not have much impact in a district with no African-American residents.[15]

TABLE 5.1

Predicting Ideology, 1972–1992

(Dependent Variable: Conservatism [Poole-Rosenthal 1st Dimension], N = 3844)

Variable	Coefficient	Standard Error
Intercept	.09	.04
Democrat	.12	.04
Proportion Black	−.30	.03
40% Black District	−.15	.04
Proportion Black × 40% Black District	.06	.07
Proportion Latino	.29	.06
Proportion Latino × Democrat	−.69	.06
South	.13	.01
South × Democrat	.07	.01
Proportion Urban	−.07	.02
Proportion 65 and Older	−.93	.08
Proportion High School Graduates × Republican	.54	.04
Deflated Median Family Income ($1,000)	−.01	.00
First Year Elected × Republican	.0034	.0005
Margin of Victory × Democrat	.03	.01
Intercept for σ	−1.92	.01
Proportion Black for σ	−.53	.09

Note: The model is similar to the standard linear regression model but it relaxes the homoscedasticity requirement. Instead of assuming a constant variance σ^2, the model lets σ^2 vary as a function of a set of explanatory variables so that $\sigma^2 = \exp(DK)$. D is a vector of explanatory variables where the first is a constant of all ones. K is a vector of parameters. In this model, proportion black is the only explanatory variable for σ^2. Maximum likelihood estimation was used to simultaneously estimate the coefficients of the independent variables and the coefficients of the variables used to predict σ^2.

Results

Table 5.1 displays the coefficients and standard errors for all variables in the model of ideology. The statistical analysis relies on 3844 observations of the ideology of representatives and characteristics of them and their districts from 1972 through 1992.[16] All of the coefficients point in the expected direction. Table 5.2 presents the same results separately for northern Democrats, southern Democrats, northern Republicans, and southern Republicans.

Calculating the Effect of Race

Calculating the overall impact of the racial composition of districts on ideology from the model outlined in the previous section requires considering both the direct and indirect effects of race on ideology. Changes in the racial composition of a district alter other nonracial demographic characteristics on congressional districts included in the model in regularly predictable ways due to the relationship between proportion black and the nonracial demographic variables. For example, as the proportion of blacks in a district rises, the median income of families in the district tends to decline. Taking into account the indirect impact of race via the nonracial demographic variables is vital when calculating the total impact of race on ideology.

The total impact of race on conservatism equals the sum of the direct and indirect impact of race on conservatism. Measuring the direct effect of race on ideology entails calculating the impact of the coefficients on the race variables (proportion black, 40% black district, proportion black × 40% black district) at different levels of proportion black. Calculating the indirect effect of race via the nonracial demographic variables is more complex. Reliable estimates of how changes in the racial composition of a district influence the nonracial demographic variables are required in order to estimate the indirect impact of race on ideology. Knowing how the nonracial demographic variables vary with changes in proportion black makes it possible to estimate the indirect impact of race on ideology by plugging these initial results into the equations presented in table 5.2.

Each demographic variable was regressed on proportion black and an intercept term in order to estimate the relationship between each of the demographic variables and proportion black. Redistricting often entails changes at the margin of districts, so data on each of the demographic variables was gathered from all U.S. Census block groups in 1990—the smallest unit for which all of the data are available. Collectively, the fifty states contain over 222,000 block groups. The large number of observations allows for estimation of the relationship between proportion black and each of the nonracial demographic variables with a high degree of certainty for each state.

Table 5.3 presents the total predicted impact of race on ideology for the South and the North (defined here as all non-Southern states) as well as for individual states in both regions. States excluded from the table either have only one congressional district or a very small number of African-American residents. Table 5.3 shows the predicted effect of a 10 percent change in the proportion of blacks on ideology for districts above and below the 40 percent black threshold as well as the predicted jump in responsiveness as districts pass the 40 percent black threshold. The scores of their representatives become more negative as African Americans win influence. Figure 5.6 graphically compares the influence of race on ideology by region and party at all levels of proportion black. The line in each graph plots the predicted impact of race on overall conservatism at different levels of proportion black.

TABLE 5.2
Predicting Ideology by Region and Party, 1972–1992
(Dependent Variable: Conservatism [Poole-Rosenthal 1st Dimension])

	Northern Democrats	Southern Democrats	Northern Republicans	Southern Republicans
Intercept	.17	.43	.17	−.004
	(.03)	(.07)	(.06)	(.069)
Proportion Black	−.24	−.44	−.36	−.21
	(.04)	(.08)	(.13)	(.08)
40% Black District	−.12	−.03		
	(.04)	(.11)		
Proportion Black × 40% Black District	.004	−.14		
	(.065)	(.22)		
Proportion Latino	−.38	−.48	.23	.18
	(.03)	(.06)	(.08)	(.13)
Proportion Urban	−.07	−.07	−.05	−.03
	(.02)	(.04)	(.04)	(.05)
Proportion 65 and Older	−.82	−.65	−1.58	−.05
	(.05)	(.21)	(.21)	(.18)
Proportion High School Graduates	.03	−.20	.57	−.11
	(.03)	(.09)	(.06)	(.09)
Deflated Median Family Income ($1,000)	−.01	−.005	−.01	.005
	(.00)	(.003)	(.00)	(.003)
First Year Elected	.0007	−.0007	.0035	.004
	(.0003)	(.0006)	(.0006)	(.001)
Margin of Victory	−.0094	.08	−.005	−.002
	(.012)	(.02)	(.019)	(.017)
Intercept for σ	−2.01	−1.74	−1.86	−2.11
	(.02)	(.06)	(.028)	(.07)
Proportion Black for σ	−.69	−.65	−.88	−1.41
	(.05)	(.24)	(.51)	(.39)
Number of Cases	1724	625	1220	275

Note: See the text or the note to table 5.1 for a description of the statistical model.

Implications

The results of the analysis have major implications regarding the role of race in American politics as well as for black representation. After examining which districts provide the highest level of representation and reviewing the white backlash theory, this section examines optimal redistricting strategies for African Americans.

TABLE 5.3

Predicted Impact of Race on Conservatism

	Total Impact of 10% Black Increase on Conservatism for Districts Less Than 40% Black		Total Impact of 10% Black Increase on Conservatism for Districts Greater Than 40% Black	Shift in Conservatism at 40% Black
	Republicans	Democrats	Democrats	Democrats
South	−.0218	−.0210	−.0533	−.2549
Alabama	−.0219	−.0320	−.0644	−.2549
Arkansas	−.0195	−.0341	−.0664	−.2549
Florida	−.0195	−.0134	−.0457	−.2549
Georgia	−.0246	−.0245	−.0568	−.2549
Louisiana	−.0223	−.0269	−.0593	−.2549
Mississippi	−.0208	−.0267	−.0591	−.2549
North Carolina	−.0222	−.0293	−.0616	−.2549
South Carolina	−.0220	−.0234	−.0557	−.2549
Tennessee	−.0215	−.0327	−.0650	−.2549
Texas	−.0227	−.0178	−.0501	−.2549
Virginia	−.0241	−.0247	−.0570	−.2549
Non-South	−.0344	−.0114	−.0199	−.1543
California	−.0241	−.0024	−.0108	−.1543
Colorado	−.0314	−.0125	−.0210	−.1543
Connecticut	−.0113	−.0036	−.0121	−.1543
Illinois	−.0326	−.0066	−.0151	−.1543
Indiana	−.0415	−.0161	−.0246	−.1543
Kentucky	−.0411	−.0202	−.0287	−.1543
Maryland	−.0300	−.0057	−.0142	−.1543
Massachusetts	−.0129	−.0046	−.0131	−.1543
Michigan	−.0362	−.0112	−.0197	−.1543
Missouri	−.0360	−.0146	−.0231	−.1543
New Jersey	−.0200	−.0010	−.0095	−.1543
New York	−.0240	−.0089	−.0173	−.1543
Ohio	−.0377	−.0107	−.0192	−.1543
Oklahoma	−.0465	−.0222	−.0307	−.1543
Pennsylvania	−.0347	−.0127	−.0212	−.1543
Washington	−.0312	−.0165	−.0250	−.1543
Wisconsin	−.0296	−.0109	−.0193	−.1543

Note: Predicted values were calculated using the coefficients presented in table 5.2. The total impact of race on conservatism equals the sum of the direct and indirect impact of race on conservatism. The direct impact was calculated using the coefficients on proportion black, 40% black district, and proportion black × 40% black district. The indirect impact was calculated in two steps. First, the relationship of proportion black to each of the nonracial demographic variables was estimated by regressing each of these variables on proportion black for the appropriate set of block groups. These estimates were then used to calculate the indirect impact of race on conservatism using the coefficients on the nonracial demographic variables presented in table 5.2.

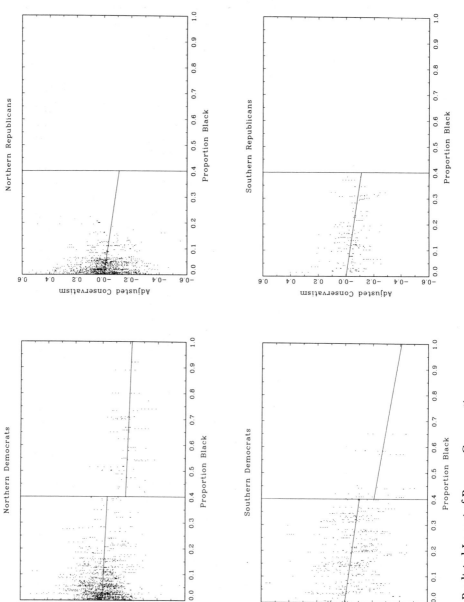

5.6. Predicted Impact of Race on Conservatism.

Black Majority Districts Provide the Highest Level of Black Representation

The expected level of black representation varies considerably depending on the racial composition of the district. Districts less than 40 percent black, the most common type of district, afford blacks the lowest level of representation, though black opinion carries some weight even in these districts. African Americans rarely win election from districts less than 40 percent black, but their influence rises with their share of the population except in districts held by northern Democrats.

Redistricting experts commonly refer to districts that concentrate black voters in areas where it is impossible to create a new black majority district as "influence districts." "Influence districts" concentrate black voters in the hope that African Americans can exert greater influence as a sizable minority in one district than as a small minority in several districts. Responsiveness to black concerns rises dramatically once a district passes the 40 percent black threshold, so new influence districts enhance black substantive representation as long as they are at least 40 percent black and do not result in the election of fewer Democrats.[17] African Americans effectively veto the election of conservative members of Congress in districts greater than 40 percent black as evidenced by the near total failure of Republicans to carry any of these districts. The chances of African-American candidates in districts between 40 and 50 percent black depend largely upon the presence of Latinos. Whites usually win 40–50 percent black districts with few Latino residents, but African Americans usually claim victory in mixed majority-minority districts.

African Americans control not only the ideology but the race of the representative in black majority districts. Moving from influence to black majority districts causes no great jump in liberalism comparable to the jump in responsiveness at the 40 percent black threshold. Representatives from black majority districts nevertheless constitute one of the most staunchly liberal contigents in the House. African Americans won the vast majority of elections in black majority districts between 1972 and 1994. Whites elected from these districts clearly serve at the pleasure of their black constituents and need strong black support to win reelection.

White Backlash Does Not Prevent Responsiveness

Several scholars and advocates of drawing more black majority districts contend that representatives actually become more conservative as the black share of the population increases in white majority districts. According to this theory, African Americans pose a greater threat to white political control as their numbers grow. Whites react against this perceived threat to white racial dominance by giving greater support to conservative candidates as the black share of the population increases. Rather than magnify black influence, heightened black population resources ignite a white backlash. The conservative backlash outweighs any potential new liberal pressures on representatives due to increases in the size of the black population. Representatives must cast more conservative roll-call votes as the black percentage of the population rises or risk defeat at the hands of the conservative white majority electorate. Moving further to the left would alienate white voters and endanger a representative's electoral coalition. The white backlash theory seems especially relevant for white Democrats who rely far more on interracial electoral coalitions than Republicans.

Previous research provides some support for the white backlash theory. V.O. Key discovered that conservative white-supremacist candidates won the most support in counties with high concentrations of blacks in his study of the pre-Voting Rights Act South. Frank Parker detailed in *Black Votes Count* how the election of the first black officials provided the first real crack in the wall of white political opposition to black political activity in Mississippi. Charles Bullock found almost no liberalization in congressional voting on racial issues as the black population increased in southern white majority districts. Mary Herring showed that black voting strength did not explain variations in voting on either social welfare or civil rights issues in her study of white state senators in Alabama, Louisiana, and Georgia. Whitby and Gilliam argues that black voting strength did not explain the heightened liberalism of southern House Democrats on racial issues. Huckfeldt and Kohfeld found that poor whites become more supportive of Republican presidential candidates as the black population rises.[18]

The results of the analysis presented here firmly refute the hypothesis that white backlash forms a solid barrier to black representation. As figure 5.6 shows, raising the proportion of blacks in the population never decreases the liberalism of the representative. White backlash may slow the rate of responsiveness to increases in black population resources, but it is not strong enough to prevent representatives from responding to increases in the voting power of their black constituents. Even districts less than 40 percent black, overwhelmingly represented by whites, demonstrate responsiveness to varying proportions of blacks in population. Increases in black support offset any rise in white conservatism. White backlash may still make representatives less responsive to African Americans than might otherwise be the case, but it does not prevent blacks from exerting any influence over their representatives.[19]

Figure 5.6 shows that representatives from a particular party never become more conservative as the black share of the population rises. White backlash, however, might manifest itself by whites electing Republicans instead of Democrats. Whites opposed to rising black power within the bi-racial and relatively liberal Democratic party might start voting for congressional candidates from the clearly conservative and overwhelmingly white Republican party. Changing racial alignments have clearly played a role in the rise of the Republicans in the South.[20] The most recent work examining the link between the percentage black in the electorate and the probability of a district electing a Democrat shows that raising the share of blacks in the population never increases the probability of a district electing a Republican.[21] White backlash does not increase the likelihood of a district electing a Republican.

The contradiction between this consistent finding of responsiveness to blacks and Key's conclusions reflects the difference between the pre– and post–Voting Rights Act era. African Americans did not have access to the franchise throughout much of the South when Key conducted his study in the 1940s. African Americans exerted no influence over their elected representatives during this period. Whites living in black majority areas had the strongest interest in maintaining the status quo and elected the most staunchly conservative, white supremacist representatives. Areas with small black populations had little to fear from black political participation. African Americans, like all citizens, can use their votes to try to elect officials responsive to their needs and concerns in the post-Voting Rights Act era. Representatives from white majority districts may try to ignore blacks as part of a strategy to win without the black vote. Most representatives, however, loathe writing off any major politically active section of their constituency. African Americans consequently gain greater influence over the politics of their member of the House as their share of the population rises. Many Democratic representatives must pay particularly strong attention to black concerns due to their dependence on biracial electoral coalitions. These representatives risk losing their party's nomination or the general election if they lose black support.

Racial Redistricting Enhances Black Representation
if the Democrats Lose No Seats

Responsiveness to African Americans increases dramatically for representatives of both regions once a district reaches the 40 percent mark. Responsiveness increases once a district crosses the 40 percent, not the 50 percent, black threshold even though African Americans rarely win election outside of majority-minority districts. This result was derived empirically. Moving the threshold above or below 40 percent black results in predicted ideology being skewed above or below the actual value of ideology. The diversity of white opinion explains why blacks exert heightened influence before attaining a majority. White opinion is less cohesively conservative than black opinion is liberal, so white liberal Democrats can usually gain enough white support to win in 40 percent black districts.

These results strongly refute Swain's argument that neither the race of a district's representative nor the percentage of blacks in the district relates to support for black interests.[22] Representatives from districts greater than 40 percent black show substantially greater responsiveness to African-American concerns than other representatives. Raising the percentage of blacks in the district above or below the 40 percent black threshold further heightens responsiveness to black concerns by southern representatives. Descriptive representation remains closely linked to substantive representation because African Americans represent the overwhelming majority of seats greater than 40 percent black but very few seats less than 40 percent black. African Americans won all 17 black majority seats in 1990, and 31 of the 32 black majority seats in 1992 and 1994. Of the seats lacking a black majority but greater than 40 percent black, blacks won 3 of 6 in 1990 and 3 of 7 in 1992 and 1994. African Americans carried only 4 of the 397 seats less than 40 percent black in 1990, and 5 of the 411 seats less than 40 percent black in 1992 and 1994. African-American representatives not only provide descriptive representation of blacks, they also provide the strongest substantive representation of black interests.

Although Swain wrongly dismisses the importance of race, she correctly analyzes that party strongly influences black substantive representation. Creating a new Republican district reduces black substantive representation more than drawing a new black district enhances it. Assuming that the party of the representative remains Democratic, increasing the black share of the population from 35 to 65 percent in 1992 would have resulted in the election of a member .23 points more liberal in the South and .16 points more liberal in other regions on the Poole-Rosenthal conservatism scale.[23] Switching from Republican to Democratic representation has a much greater effect. Holding all other variables constant, northern Democratic representatives elected in 1992 are predicted to cast roll-call votes about .62 points more liberal than their Republican counterparts—an enormous change on a scale that only ranges from around −.9 (e.g., Barbara Boxer) to .8 (e.g., Bill Archer). Even southern Democrats should vote .52 points less conservative than their Republican rivals.[24]

Taking party into account in estimating the effect of racial redistricting on black substantive representation is absolutely critical because creating a new Republican district reduces black substantive representation more than drawing a new black majority district enhances it. Proponents of racial redistricting ignore the close connection between race and party at peril of injuring black substantive representation. Racial redistricting would not help the Republicans win more seats if race and partisanship showed no consistent relationship. The relationship between race and party in the South, the location of all but one of the new black districts drawn during the 1990 redistricting cycle, is particularly strong. Ninety-one percent of southern blacks but only 35 percent of southern whites voted Democratic in the 1994 congressional elections according to the CBS/New York Times poll. No group votes more consistently Democratic than African Americans, so concentrating African Americans in a district greatly aids Democratic chances of victory in that district. Concentrating black voters in one district necessitates reducing the black population, and the number of Democratic voters, in surrounding districts. Many white Democrats depend upon a base of minority voters to win reelection. Republicans joined with African Americans and Latinos to push for the creation of new majority-minority districts during the 1990 redistricting round because they hoped that packing black voters in a few districts would aid the election of more Republicans from the remaining districts.[25] Placing a ceiling of around 55 percent black on new black majority districts can help minimize the potential damage to black substantive representation without seriously jeopardizing African-American control.

Racial redistricting strongly advantages African Americans as long as the partisan composition of a state's delegation remains unchanged. Reconfiguring two adjoining 30 percent black districts so that one district has a black majority and the other has few blacks will clearly increase black descriptive and substantive representation if the number of Democrats does not decline. The new configuration magnifies overall responsiveness to blacks by increasing the number of districts greater than 40 percent black by one. Raising the percentage of African Americans in one district from 30 to greater than 50 percent also substantially increases the likelihood that the district will increase black descriptive representation by electing a black representative to the House.[26]

Racial Redistricting Undermines Black Representation in the South but Not the North

Northern Democrats appear almost shockingly less responsive to changes in the black share of the population than other representatives. Southern Democrats cast more liberal roll-call votes as the percentage of African Americans increases both above and below the 40 percent black threshold. Northern Democratic responsiveness rises substantially only when a district crosses the 40 percent black threshold. Changes in the racial composition of the district above and below this threshold do not greatly alter the degree of responsiveness by northern Democrats. Even Republicans from both North and South show more responsiveness to changes in the share of the black popularion below the 40 percent black threshold.

Assessments of the relative sensitivity of Democrats compared to Republicans to variations in the African-American share of the population have only a limited value because Republicans rarely represent districts greater than 30 percent black.[27] Forty-five of the sixty-four southern Republicans elected to the House in 1994 represented districts less than 15 percent black. Sixteen won election from districts 15–25 percent black, and three carried districts 25–30 percent black. Northern Republicans are even more likely to represent districts under 15 percent black. Studies of the link between the racial composition of districts and ideology should focus primarily on Democrats since Republicans usually win election from overwhelmingly white districts while Democrats represent districts with widely varying racial compositions.

Variations among the individual states of each region help confirm the substantial regional differences in responsiveness by Democrats. Democrats from Florida and Texas, the least culturally southern of the southern states, show less responsiveness to changes in the proportion of blacks above and below the 40 percent black threshold than other southern Democrats. Democrats from Kentucky and Oklahoma, the most culturally southern of the northern states, show greater responsiveness to changes in the proportion of blacks than Democrats from any other northern state.

At first glance, these results seem bizarre. Northern representatives have historically demonstrated greater responsiveness to blacks than southern representatives. Although northern representatives could hardly be viewed as paragons of responsiveness to blacks, prior to the passage of the Civil Rights Act of 1964 and the Voting Rights Act of 1965, most southern representatives actively worked to maintain white supremacy—a system that brutally enforced the economic and political subjugation of African Americans in the South. Northern representatives successfully fought for passage of these acts over the vehement objections of most southern representatives. Unlike most southern blacks, northern blacks could vote and participate in politics long before the passage of the Voting Rights Act of 1965.

Regional differences in where African Americans live and in the political ideology of whites explain these seemingly odd results. Concentrating black voters into black majority districts is almost impossible outside of large central cities in the North. The creation of new black majority districts requires that surrounding districts lose liberal black voters. This decline in black voting strength usually does not imperil the electoral chances of northern Democrats because other central city residents who tend to support Democratic candidates replace the lost black voters. Jews and non-Cuban Latinos—the only two ethnic groups who support Democratic candidates in percentages approaching that of blacks—compose a disproportionate share of the non-black population in northern metropolitan areas. Seventy-eight percent of Jews and 70 percent of Latinos voted Democratic in 1994 according to the

CBS/New York Times poll.[28] Racial redistricting consequently causes the Democrats to suffer few losses in the North.

The concentration of Jews, a relatively small population group, in metropolitan areas with Democratic representatives minimizes the potential negative effect of racial redistricting on Democratic electoral chances and black substantive representation in the North. Eighty-two percent of the northern Jewish population lives in states with black representatives. Table 5.4 reveals that the overwhelming majority of Jews living in states with black Democratic representatives live in the same metropolitan areas as these representatives. Few African Americans and Jews may actually live in the same neighborhoods, but Jews live in close enough proximity to African Americans that excluding white voters from a congressional district tends to increase the Jewish population of other districts in the area. Racial segregation undoubtedly makes it more likely that racial redistricting separates African-American and Jewish voters into adjoining districts rather than lumping them together in the same district. Fifty-three percent of northern black representatives elected in 1994 held seats that adjoin districts represented by Jewish Democrats.

Table 5.5 shows that the metropolitan areas that contain districts represented by black Democrats also contain sizable Latino populations. Excluding nonblacks from some districts makes other districts more Latino and helps protect against Democratic losses due to the creation of new black majority districts. Despite Cuban-American enclaves in the North, most Cuban Americans live in Florida, so Cuban preferences, unique among Latinos, for Republican over Democratic candidates usually do not harm northern Democrats. Cuban Americans living in the North may prefer Democrats more often than Cuban Americans from the South. Robert Menendez, the sole Cuban-American representative from the North, caucuses with the Democrats.

White Christians who live in northern cities vote Democratic at a higher rate than their counterparts elsewhere. Fifty-two percent of Catholics voted for Democratic congressional candidates compared to 34 percent of white Protestants according to the 1994 CBS/New York Times poll. Catholics reside disproportionately in northern metropolitan areas, so confessional differences in voting patterns help mitigate the effect of concentrating African Americans in black majority districts in northern cities.

Racial redistricting could hardly have a more different effect in the South. Racial redistricting in the South usually harms black substantive representation. Contrasting regional residential patterns among African Americans and voting preferences among whites explain the differential impact of racial redistricting in the South compared to the North. Individual southern metropolitan areas do not contain enough blacks to support an entire black district, so racial redistricting usually requires connecting several urban

TABLE 5.4

1994 Jewish Population in Northern Metropolitan Areas with Black Democrats

State	Metropolitan Area	Jews	Percent of Jews in State	Smaller Unit	Jews	Percent of Jews in Metro Area
California	Los Angeles-Anaheim-Riverside CMSA	590,000	64	N/A		
	San Francisco-Oakland-San Jose CMSA	216,000	23	Alameda and Contra Costa counties	54,500	25
			87			
Illinois	Chicago-Gary-Lake Country CMSA	263,000	98	N/A		
Maryland	Baltimore MSA	105,000	50	City and County	94,500	90
	Washington, D.C. MSA	104,500	49	Montgomery and Prince Georges counties	104,500	100
			99			
Michigan	Detroit-Ann Arbor CMSA	99,000	93	N/A		
Missouri	St. Louis MSA	54,000	88	City and County	53,500	99
New Jersey	New York-Northern NJ-Long Island CMS	358,000	82	Essex, Hudson, and Union counties	118,540	33
New York	New York-Northern NJ-Long Island CMS	1,450,000	88	New York City	1,048,900	72
Ohio	Cleveland-Akron-Lorain CMSA	71,000	55	Cuyahoga County	65,000	92
Pennsylvania	Philadelphia PMSA	250,000	76	N/A		

Source: "Jewish Population in the United States, 1994" in the American Jewish Yearbook 1995 (New York: American Jewish Committee, 1995), 181–206.
Note: Excludes Jews in metropolitan area but out of state since districts cannot cross state boundaries.

TABLE 5.5

1990 Hispanic Population in Northern Metropolitan Areas with Black Democrats

State	Metropolitan Area	Hispanics	Percent of Hispanics in State	Smaller Unit	Percent of Hispanics in Metro Area
California	LA-Anaheim-Riverside CMSA	3,351,242	44		
	LA-Long Beach PMSA	1,617,447	21	LA County	100
	San Francisco-Oakland-San Jose CMSA	970,403	13	Alameda and Contra Costa counties	28
	Oakland PMSA	273,087	4		
Illinois	Chicago-Gary-Lake County CMSA	839,458	93		
	Chicago PMSA	734,827	81	Cook County	83
Maryland	Baltimore MSA	30,160	24	City and County	52
	Washington, D.C. MSA	89,587	72	Montgomery and Prince Georges counties	96
Michigan	Detroit-Ann Arbor CMSA	90,947	45		
	Detroit PMSA	85,216	42	Wayne County	59
Missouri	St. Louis MSA	18,835	31	City and County	79
New Jersey	NY-Northern NJ-Long Island CMSA	627,684	85	Essex, Hudson and Union counties	56
	Jersey City PMSA	183,465	25		
	Newark PMSA	188,299	25		
New York	NY-Northern NJ-Long Island CMSA	2,076,435	94		
	New York PMSA	1,889,662	85	New York City	95
Ohio	Cleveland-Akron-Lorain CMSA	52,997	38		
	Cleveland PMSA	33,921	24	Cuyahoga County	93
Pennsylvania	Philadelphia PMSA	121,008	52	Philadelphia	74

Source: 1990 United States Census.

Note: Excludes Hispanics in metropolitan area but out of state since districts cannot cross state boundaries.

centers with rural black areas. The relative dispersion of African Americans means that racial redistricting in southern contexts results in sprawling black districts that contrast sharply with the relatively compact black districts in northern states.

Few Jews or non-Cuban Latinos live in the South outside of Florida and Texas—the two states that deviate most from the overall pattern for the region as a whole. Only 24 percent of white born-again Christians, who live disproportionately in the South, supported Democratic congressional candidates in 1994. The relative conservatism of southern whites compared to northern whites living in central cities causes racial redistricting to have radically different consequences in the South and the North. Liberal black southern voters do not live in close proximity to numerous members of other groups who vote heavily Democratic as in the North, so packing black voters into black districts makes surrounding districts more likely to elect Republicans with devestating consequences for black substantive representation. Most southern Republicans show scant interest in supporting policies favored by most African Americans.

Unlike their northern counterparts, southern white Democrats depend heavily on biracial coalitions to win elections. Successful southern white Democrats perform a precarious balancing act, trying to please white and black voters. Democrats need fewer white votes as the black share of the populations grows and so they can cast more liberal roll-call votes on racial and economic issues without fear of losing reelection. Racial redistricting concentrates black votes in black districts and forces white Democratic representatives to shift to the Right in search of white conservative votes. The district goes Republican if white Democrats lose enough of their black base—the most reliable source of Democratic votes. The result is a trade-off between descriptive and substantive representation in the South, though not in the North. Ironically, southern representatives respond more to changes in the black share of the vote precisely because of the high salience of race in the South compared to northern central cities.[29]

Conclusion

Racial redistricting has been the centerpiece of the strategy to increase black representation under the Voting Rights Act. The results of the statistical analysis of the link between race and ideology indicate that respresentatives 'become more responsive to black interests as the black population rises. Racial redistricting clearly works to make individual representatives more responsive to black concerns because responsiveness increases dramatically once a district crosses the 40 percent black threshold. Representatives elected from black majority districts attend more closely to black concerns in their roll-call voting behavior than other representatives. African-American representatives, who represent all of the voting-age majority black districts but few non-majority-minority districts, provide the highest level of substantive representation in addition to descriptive representation. African Americans can wholly control the political process in black majority districts, so this high level of responsiveness makes perfect sense. Any politician who ignores the interests of the black community in black majority districts probably will have a short career as that district's representative. The creation of black influence districts similarly augments black representation within a particular district if the district's black population exceeds 40 percent.

Representatives differ by party and region in their sensitivity to changes in the percentage of blacks. Southern Democrats are highly responsive to changes in the percentage of blacks above and below the 40 percent black threshold, while northern Democrats exhibit little change in their roll-call voting behavior. Contrasts in the dispersion of blacks and the ideology of whites explain these regional differences in responsiveness to blacks. In the South, racial redistricting packs black liberal voters into districts and makes the surrounding districts more white and conservative. White Democrats in these districts must vote conservatively or risk losing their seats. Racial redistricting results in the election of Republicans if the shift is large enough to alter the partisan balance of the district. In the North, large numbers of white Democrats live in close proximity to blacks, so racial redistricting does not usually make surrounding districts more likely to elect Republicans.

Creating new black majority districts consequently results in the election of more African Americans but congressional delegations as a whole are less likely to support policies favored by blacks in the South, but not the North. The next chapter explores how the creation of new black majority districts in the South in the 1990s increased the number of African Americans and Republicans elected at the expense of white Democrats and aggregate black substantive representation.

6

RACIAL REDISTRICTING AND PUBLIC POLICY

THIS CHAPTER applies the results from chapter 5 in order to measure the aggregate impact of drawing new black majority districts on the substantive representation of African Americans in the House of Representatives. Racial redistricting prior to 1990 had little impact on the partisan makeup of the House or black substantive representation. The pressure to create ever more black majority districts in the 1990s resulted in the election of more Republicans and a consequent decline in black substantive representation following the 1992 elections.

This chapter gradually develops this argument. After exploring the basic tension between advancing black descriptive representation, which necessitates creating new black majority districts, and promoting black substantive representation, which requires drawing new Democratic districts, the next section turns to strategies for minimizing the conflict between these two goals. The chapter then analyzes the effect of racial redistricting on black substantive representation in the 1980s and 1990s.

Racial redistricting did not reduce black substantive representation in the 1980s, but it reduced the number of representatives favorably disposed to black interests in the 1990s. The creation of new black majority districts in states that did not enact Democratic gerrymanders largely accounts for the moderate decline in support for most legislation favored by blacks between the Congresses elected in 1990 and 1992. Liberal bills with only a small chance of passage in either the pre- or postredistricting Congresses were the only type of legislation to gain support in the House due to racial redistricting.

Maximizing Black Substantive Representation through Redistricting

The previous chapter's analysis of the link between race, party, and ideology suggests clear guidelines for mapmakers desiring to enhance black substantive representation. Democrats vote for policies favored by African Americans markedly more often than Republicans. Maximizing the number of seats held by Democrats consequently increases aggregate support for black interests in the House. Transferring African Americans from one district to another raises the overall liberalism of a state's delegation only if the total number of districts greater than 40 percent black increases and the number of districts won by Democrats does not decline. Reducing the number of Democratic districts harms black substantive representation substantially more than drawing a new 40 percent black district increases it. Mapmakers desiring solely to maximize black substantive representation should give priority to protecting Democratic seats over drawing additional districts greater than 40 percent black.

Maximizing Descriptive and Substantive Representation Conflict

Black majority districts assure the election of black representatives but impede efforts to maximize black substantive representation. Utilizing the same African-American population base to create a new Democratic district or a second 40 percent black district results in greater substantive representation gains. Raising the black share of population from 40 percent to 55 or 65 percent does not increase overall responsiveness to African Americans. Concentrating black voters in black majority districts actually undermines black substantive representation if it prevents redistricters from placing black voters in districts where they aid the election of an additional Democrat or raise the black share of the population above 40 percent.

Maximizing black substantive representation exacts a heavy price in terms of descriptive representation. No Republicans currently represent districts greater than 30 percent black, so maximizing the number of Democratic seats, and thus black substantive representation, would entail dismantling many black majority districts. Concentrating blacks to a greater extent wastes black votes that could contribute to the construction of additional Democratic districts. Districts might need to be more than 30 percent black to assure the election of a Democrat in parts of the country with exceptionally high levels of racial polarization. Black majority districts might actually aid southern Democrats if the percentage of whites voting Republican continues to increase. Democratic candidates might find it impossible to win outside of black majority districts if few whites vote Democratic. The general implication is nevertheless clear. Black majority districts usually conflict with efforts to maximize African-American substantive representation. Doing the utmost to advance black interests necessitates destroying most black majority districts.

The costs of incremental gains in substantive representation in terms of descriptive representation should not be lightly dismissed. Alabama, Florida, North Carolina, South Carolina, and Virginia elected African-American representatives in 1992 for the first time since Reconstruction thanks to racial redistricting. Nonblack representatives can ardently support black interests but they cannot actually be black. African-American voters often feel more comfortable approaching a black representative for constituent service or about a public policy concern.[1] The election of white ethnic representatives visibly symbolized their clout and status as well as their assimilation into the American polity. African-American efforts to elect blacks to public office are both utterly understandable and American.

Packing more black voters into districts that already have a black voting majority wastes black votes that could be better used in advancing either descriptive or substantive representation in other districts. Some black politicians and activists support creating black districts with overwhelming black supermajorities in order to minimize white influence in black districts even though raising the black percentage in a district from 65 to 85 percent does little to advance black substantive representation. African-American representatives from 65 percent black districts already form part of the most liberal wing of the House. Making a solid liberal into an ultraliberal by increasing the black proportion in the district's population does nothing to advance the interests of black voters. Creating a district with an African-American supermajority comes at the cost of losing the opportunity to place some black voters in an adjoining district and gaining influence over that district's representative. Supermajority districts require that African Americans forgo the opportunity to assure the election of a moderate instead of a conservative or a liberal instead of a moderate.

White influence in black majority districts seems to affect the style, more than the substance, of black representatives. White voters prefer black candidates with a more conciliatory, nonracial approach over black candidates with a militant style. White voters occasionally cast decisive votes in Democratic primaries between strongly matched black candidates in black majority districts. John Lewis faced off against Julian Bond for the black majority Fifth District of Georgia in 1986. Lewis lost the black vote but won the Democratic primary runoff by carrying 80 percent of the vote in majority white precincts. Although Lewis seemingly had more biracial appeal and Bond was perceived by some as a "jet-setter," the two rivals differed little on substance.

Republicans, avowed opponents of every other affirmative action policy and many other programs favored by African Americans, formed alliances with blacks and Latinos to push for the creation of mew majority-minority districts during the 1990 redistricting cycle because they hoped that packing black voters in a few districts would result in the election of more Republicans from the remaining districts. Republicans, and indeed Democrats, know that many white Democratic representatives depend upon a base of minority voters to win reelection repeatedly. Republican strategists thought that by removing this base of black voter support, Republican challengers could defeat more of these incumbents or at least that Republican candidates would have a greater chance of winning their seats when the incumbent retires. Republicans further expected that drawing new majority-minority districts would disrupt the framework of old plans that they viewed as biased toward the Democrats.[2]

African Americans suffer a net loss in substantive representation even if Republicans post a net gain of just one seat from the creation of a new black influence or black majority district. The advance in descriptive representation may somewhat mitigate these substantive losses. African-American voters support the election of black representatives not just to gain a new role model, but because they believe that black representatives will work harder for real substantive gains for their community. The election of more Republicans makes it more difficult for African-American representatives to achieve these gains. Republican gains in 1994 severely undermined congressional support for many government programs supported by African Americans. To the extent that racial redistricting aided the Republicans in winning solid control of the House, it had the paradoxical effect of assuring a great reduction in the influence of the Congressional Black Caucus at the same time as its membership expanded dramatically thanks to the influx of new black representatives elected due to racial redistricting.

Jointly Maximizing Descriptive and Substantive Representation

So far, the discussion has focused on the ideal manner for maximizing black substantive representation without regard to other concerns, particularly descriptive representation. Under ideal conditions for substantive representation, the number of black majority districts, vital for the election of more than token numbers of African Americans to the House, would inevitably decline to make way for more Democratic districts with nonblack majorities. Enforcement of the Voting Rights Act has concentrated far more on improving the descriptive representation of African Americans through the creation of new majority black districts than on the underlying goal of enhancing black substantive representation.

Cooperation between black legislators and white Democrats to pass redistricting plans that create new majority black districts without reducing the overall proportion of Democrats in the state's congressional delegation minimizes the fundamental conflict between improving black descriptive and substantive representation. Both sides had strong incentives to participate in such a cooperative effort during the 1990 redistricting round. African-American Democratic legislators strongly desired the creation of new black majority districts if only to open up future avenues for personal career advancement. Black and white Democrats had strong incentives to work together to craft redistricting plans despite the conflict between creating new black districts and protecting white Democrats. African-American Democrats did not want the Republicans to benefit from racial redistricting. The past willingness of courts, often viewed as controlled by the Republicans, to impose plans with new majority-minority districts encouraged white Democrats to cooperate in passing a redistricting plan that created new majority black districts and but guarded their own interests at the same time. The Voting Rights Act effectively forced white Democrats to negotiate with black Democrats over new redistricting plans.[3]

Drafting a plan that both creates new black seats and protects white incumbent Democrats is not as impossible as it appears at first glance. Black and white Democrats colluded in 1990 to pass plans in several states that promote exactly these goals. With the aid of computers, redistricting experts can carefully tailor districts to produce many different outcomes.[4] Constructing plans that promote the election of more blacks without decimating black substantive representation requires following two rules. First, pack as many white Republicans as possible into as few districts as possible. Just as packing blacks into a few districts wastes black votes, cramming Republicans into a few districts wastes Republican votes. Wasting Republican votes strengthens the Democrats and aids black substantive representation.

Second, packing black voters should be avoided at all costs in order to allow for the most efficient use of black voting strength. Fifty-five percent black districts should elect African Americans to the House in most parts of the country. Raising the proportion of blacks above 55 percent wastes black votes that could be used to shore up Democratic support in other districts. Lastly, if it is possible without endangering any Democrats, problack mapmakers should try to boost majority white districts above the 40 percent threshold in order to further boost black substantive representation. This last suggestion is probably very difficult to implement once new black districts have been created and white Democrats have gained a measure of political protection under the new plan.

The major drawback of plans that follow these guidelines is that they tend to result in extremely unattractive maps that split political boundaries and push the contiguity requirement to the limit. Redistricting always involves trade-offs and the cost of drawing Democratic gerrymanders with new black districts tends to be compactness and contiguity. Of course, many redistricting plans fail to achieve compactness for reasons that have little to do with race.[5] The current Massachusetts districts wander crazily around the state in an effort to satisfy the interests of both the Democrats in the state legislature and the Republican governor. Compactness may mask other types of redistricting chicanery. Arizona's plan for the 1980s looked reasonably compact on the map. This Republican gerrymander packed Democrats into one district by connecting the Democratic sections of Yuma, Tucson, and Phoenix across hundreds of miles of empty desert.

The Minimal Aggregate Effect of Racial Redistricting on Black Substantive Representation in the 1980s

The Supreme Court ruled in *Mobile v. Bolden* that plaintiffs wishing to prove a Section 2 violation of the Voting Rights Act must prove not only that the plan had the effect of discriminating against minorities, but that the state intended to discriminate when it adopted the plan. Congress overturned this decision and reinstated the effects standard when it amended and renewed the Voting Rights Act in 1982. The Supreme Court upheld the amendments in 1986 in *Thornburg v. Gingles.* Racial redistricting consequently did not get into full swing until the 1990 redistricting round; states created only four new black districts during the 1980s. Three of these four cases anticipated the pressure brought to bear under the Voting Rights Act to create new black districts. Judges ordered Georgia, Louisiana, and Mississippi to each create one new district during the 1980s and to later increase the percentage of blacks in the Georgia and Mississippi districts. New York drew one new black majority district during its regular redistricting after the 1980 census.

Redrawing the lines caused no long-term shift in the partisan balance in the congressional delegations of any of these states because the existing districts were already at least 40 percent black and situated in heavily Democratic areas. Popular white Democratic incumbents continued to win election with little opposition in three of the new black districts even after the district gained a black voting majority. Wyche Fowler represented a majority black district in Atlanta until his successful senatorial campaign in 1986. Lindy Boggs easily defeated black primary challengers in her New Orleans-based district until she voluntarily retired in 1990. Joe Addabbo held on in his Queens, New York, district until his death in 1986.

The Second District of Mississippi district formed the one exception to this pattern. Mississippi obliterated the state's traditional Delta district as part of the state's massive resistance redistricting plan that assured white dominance in all districts. The legislature reestablished the black majority district centered on the Delta under pressure from federal courts and the Voting Rights Act, but it successfully subverted the intent of the act by artfully crafting a district technically majority black, but majority white in voting-age population. This new "black majority" district elected conservative white Republican Webb Franklin to the House in 1982. Franklin won reelection in 1984 even though the federal courts forced Mississippi to increase the black percentage in its population prior to the election. African-American Mike Espy defeated Frankln in 1986 by increasing black turnout and winning slightly greater white support.[6]

The creation of these four new districts enhanced black descriptive and substantive representation. The reconfiguring of districts in these states did not change the partisan composition of their congressional delegation or harm incumbents of either party in surrounding districts. Joe Addabbo's home borough of Queens, New York, lost one Democratic representative, but declining population and reapportionment, rather than redistricting, explain the loss.

The Negative Aggregate Effect of Racial Redistricting on Black Substantive Representation in the 1990s

Two cases, Alabama and North Carolina, demonstrate that creating new majority black districts can either hinder or advance black substantive representation. Racial redistricting benefits the Republicans and harms black substantive representation unless Democrats successfully craft a partisan gerrymander to mitigate the negative effects of racial redistricting.

Two Contrasting Cases: Alabama and North Carolina

ALABAMA: RACIAL REDISTRICTING ADVANTAGES THE REPUBLICANS

Redistricting in Alabama worked exactly as the Republicans hoped. This outcome is not altogether surprising since the Republicans suggested the lines imposed by a federal court.[7] The major changes occurred in the Sixth and Seventh Districts (see fig. 6.1). The Seventh District shed most of its white suburban Republican territory around Birmingham to the Sixth District and picked up most of Birmingham's black Democratic precincts in exchange. The new Seventh gained additional new black precincts around the state capitol of Montgomery from the Second District. Redistricting increased the black population of the Seventh District from 33 to 68 percent. The black percentage of the Sixth District's population plummeted from 34 to 9 percent. Redistricting similarly reduced the black share of the population in the Second District from 32 to 24 percent.

Incumbent Claude Harris, a white Democrat, decided to retire rather than seek reelection from the majority black Seventh District. Earl Hilliard became the first African American to represent Alabama in the House since the close of Reconstruction by winning election from the Seventh District in 1992. White incumbent Democrat Ben Erdreich fought for his seat despite the unfavorable boundary changes. Despite a strong effort, Erdreich failed to overcome the strong Republican advantage in a Sixth District denuded of most of its African-American voters. Republican Terry Everett defeated Democrat George Wallace Jr., by a margin of 3,571 votes in the open Second

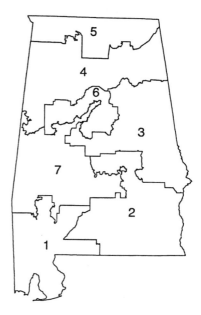

1990 Plan			1992 Plan	
Name	Percent Black		Name	Percent Black
1 Callahan (R)	31		1 Callahan (R)	28
2 Dickinson (R)	31		2 Everett (R)	24
3 Browder (D)	28		3 Browder (D)	26
4 Bevill (D)	7		4 Bevill (D)	7
5 Cramer (D)	14		5 Cramer (D)	15
6 Erdreich (D)	34		6 Bachus (R)	9
7 Harris (D)	33		7 Hilliard (D)	68

6.1. Alabama Congressional Districts in 1990 and 1992.
 Source: Map © Election Data Services, Inc.

District. The Democrats would have picked up the open Second District in 1992 if redistricting had not reduced the number of black voters in the district. Confirming the results of the 1992 elections, incumbents won all of Alabama's congressional seats in 1994.

Racial redistricting shifted the partisan balance of the Alabama delegation and diminished black substantive representation. Packing black voters into the Seventh District wasted Democratic voting strength and cost the Democrats the Second and Sixth Districts. The Second, Sixth, and Seventh Districts now elect one liberal black Democrat and two conservative white Republicans instead of three moderate white Democrats. Alabama's redistricting plan advanced black descriptive representation at the expense of black substantive representation. Alabama blacks can count on one sure vote on the floor of the House in the form of African-American Earl Hilliard, but African Americans will find it exceedingly difficult to gain the vote of Republicans Spencer Bachus or Terry Everett. Bachus and Everett have few blacks in their districts and little reason to worry about black concerns. Racial redistricting in Alabama increased the size of the opposition to legislation supported by African Americans by two votes.

NORTH CAROLINA: RACIAL REDISTRICTING AND PROTECTING DEMOCRATS

North Carolina found itself in the enviable position of having its congressional delegation increased from eleven to twelve after the 1990 census. Democrats entirely controlled the redistricting process even though North Carolina's governor was a Republican because North Carolina governors lack the power to veto legislation. North Carolina had no majority black districts and no blacks represented its people in the Congress prior to redistricting (see fig. 6.2). Intense competition characterized North Carolina congressional elections throughout the 1980s. Congressional seats regularly changed parties in many North Carolina districts while the rest of the nation bemoaned the permanent Congress and the seemingly undefeatable incumbent.

North Carolina Democrats wanted to bolster their party's marginal incumbents during the redistricting process. They faced the dilemma of protecting incumbent white Democrats while drafting new black majority districts to satisfy the Voting Rights Act as interpreted by the Justice Department. Partisan Democrats solved this problem by skillfully crafting a redistricting plan designed to meet these twin goals. North Carolina's plan stands out as a truly creative work of art (see fig. 6.2). The districts regularly violate county and town boundaries and meander all over the map in shapes no salamander could hope to approximate. Districts 1 and 3, and 6 and 12 bisect each other repeatedly; each district is at times contiguous only at a point.

Two majority black districts arose out of the redistricting process. Legislators carved the First District, which elected African-American Eva Clayton in 1992, largely out of the seat of retiring white Democrat Walter Jones. Eva Clayton's victory in the First marked the election of the first woman from North Carolina as well as the first black representative since George White left the House in 1901.[8] Continuing this pattern of success, Clayton won election as president of the large House freshman class in 1992.[9]

Democratic state legislators proved their ingenuity in the drafting of North Carolina's second black majority district. The Justice Department refused to preclear North Carolina's original redistricting plans on the grounds that the legislature should have drawn a second majority nonwhite district. The department hinted that North Carolina could solve this problem by

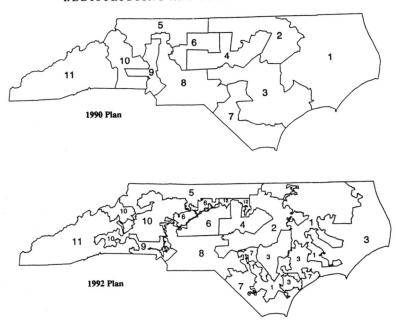

Name	Percent Black		Name	Percent Black
1 Jones (D)	35		1 **Clayton (D)**	57
2 Valentine (D)	40		2 Valentine (D)	22
3 Lancaster (D)	27		3 Lancaster (D)	21
4 Price (D)	20		4 Price (D)	20
5 Neal (D)	16		5 Neal (D)	15
6 *Coble (R)*	21		6 *Coble (R)*	7
7 Rose (D)	27		7 Rose (D)	19
8 Hefner (D)	20		8 Hefner (D)	23
9 *McMillan (R)*	23		9 *McMillan (R)*	9
10 *Ballenger (R)*	11		10 *Ballenger (R)*	5
11 *Taylor (R)*	5		11 *Taylor (R)*	7
			12 **Watt (D)**	57

6.2. North Carolina Congressional Districts in 1990 and 1992.
Source: Map © Election Data Services, Inc.

drawing a new majority black and Lumbee Indian district in southeastern
North Carolina. Republicans loved this idea because it concentrated more
Democratic voters and might have cost incumbent white Democrat Charlie
Rose his seat. The Democrats ingeniously solved this new problem by drawing a new majority black district in the central portion of the state. Following
Interstate 85, the Twelfth District connects the black communities of Gastonia, Charlotte, Winston-Salem, Greensboro, and Durham. According to
reports, anyone driving along the highway with both of their car doors wide
open would kill most of the district's residents. The Department of Justice

approved this plan, and the Twelfth District sent African-American Melvin Watt to Congress in 1992.[10]

North Carolina created two new majority black districts but white incumbents did not fare badly in the process. All of the incumbents in the white majority districts sought reelection and all of them won in avowedly anti-incumbent 1992. Packing Republicans into a few very safe Republican districts helped Democrats achieve their goals, so no Republican incumbent was endangered by the plan. Some white Democrats still had marginal seats, but a couple saw their reelection prospects enhanced. The Democrats did not waste black votes by packing too many black voters into the new majority black districts. African Americans compose 57 percent of the population in both Clayton's and Watt's districts. When white majority districts had to lose black population, Democrats replaced the blacks with rural white Democrats, rather than suburban white Republicans. North Carolina Democrats improved their majority in the state's congressional delegation from 7–4 to 8–4 in the 1992 elections.

African Americans greatly benefited from the redistricting plan in the 1992 elections by any measurement. The black community went from having no descriptive representation to two representatives. The legislature improved black substantive representation by simultaneously increasing the ratio of Democrats to Republicans and drawing a greater number of at least 40 percent black districts. Tim Valentine's 40 percent black district had the highest share of blacks in the state prior to redistricting. African Americans constituted only 22 percent of the population in Valentine's district after redistricting, but both of the two new black majority districts easily exceeded the 40 percent threshold for a boost in black substantive representation.

The 1994 elections revealed that even clever gerrymanders cannot necessarily protect white moderate Democrats against losses due to racial redistricting over the long term. African Americans are more reliably loyal than other Democratic constituencies so concentrating African-American voters heightens the impact of electoral swings against the Democrats outside of black majority districts. North Carolina Democrats lost four seats in 1994 despite the best efforts of the Democratic legislature to draw two new black districts without weakening their hold on the remaining seats. Racial redistricting accounts for at least two of these losses. Democrats probably would have won both the Second and Third Districts if they had retained the same percentage of blacks as prior to redistricting. The percentage of blacks excised during redistricting exceeds the Republican margin of victory in both districts. The legislature might have further prevented incumbent Democrat David Price's narrow defeat in the Fourth District if it had focused its creativity in districting solely on protecting Democrats.

Aggregate National Effect of Racial Redistricting

The Alabama and North Carolina examples demonstrate that racial redistricting does not inherently have either a positive or a negative effect on black substantive representation. Drawing a new black district in Alabama advanced black descriptive representation at the cost to black substantive representation of one less Democratic district. Clever Democratic drafters managed to improve temporarily both descriptive and substantive representation of African Americans in North Carolina by increasing both the number of black majority and Democratic districts. Other states, such as Louisiana and Texas, had greater success in preserving Democratic hegemony over the long term through gerrymandering. White and black Democrats working together may avert the negative aspects of racial redistricting for black substantive representation if the Democrats control the redistricting process.

Table 6.1 aggregates the impact of individual state plans in order to discover the total partisan and ideological effects of creating new black majority districts. The table divides the nine states that gained new black majority districts through redistricting between 1990 and 1992 into two categories: states that enacted Democratic gerrymanders, like North Carolina, and states that did not, like Alabama. Democrats were split into moderate and liberal categories based upon the past voting records of incumbent representatives and their Poole-Rosenthal scores. African Americans and Latinos account for the bulk of the Democrats classified as liberal. Republicans were not separated into two groups because virtually all of them may safely be catagorized as conservatives.[11]

The number of black representatives rose from four to seventeen in the nine states with new black districts in 1992. The number of Latino representatives increased from five to seven in these same states. Racial redistricting accounts completely for the election of these new black and Latino representatives. All of the new black and Latino representatives won election from districts with majorities of people of the same race or ethnicity as themselves. The number of liberal Democrats elected from these states jumped from sixteen to twenty-nine—a 10 percent increase—thanks almost exclusively to racial redistricting and the influx of numerous new African-American representatives. The percentage of liberal representatives more than doubled, from 12 to 25 percent in states that adopted Democratic gerrymanders. Changes in the percentage of liberals reflected more the creation of new black districts than the election of new Democrats.

Racial redistricting decimated the number of white moderate Democrats serving in the House. States that failed to enact Democratic gerrymanders designed to protect white incumbents saw a particularly sharp decline in the

TABLE 6.1
Representatives by Partisanship and Congress

	102nd Congress, elected 1990			103rd Congress, elected 1992		
	Republicans	Moderate Democrats	Liberal Democrats	Republicans	Moderate Democrats	Liberal Democrats
DEMOCRATIC GERRYMANDERS:						
Louisiana	4	3	1	3	2	2
North Carolina	4	7	0	4	6	2
Texas	8	13	6	9	13	8
Virginia	4	6	0	4	4	3
	20 (36%)	29 (52%)	7 (12%)	20 (33%)	25 (42%)	15 (25%)
OTHER STATES:						
Alabama	2	5	0	3	3	1
Florida	10	5	4	13	5	5
Georgia	1	8	1	4	4	3
Maryland	3	1	4	4	0	4
South Carolina	2	4	0	3	2	1
	18 (36%)	23 (46%)	9 (18%)	27 (49%)	14 (25%)	14 (25%)
TOTAL	38 (36%)	52 (49%)	16 (15%)	47 (41%)	39 (34%)	29 (25%)

	104th Congress, elected 1994			Net Change, 1990–1994		
	Republicans	Moderate Democrats	Liberal Democrats	Republicans	Moderate Democrats	Liberal Democrats
DEMOCRATIC GERRYMANDERS:						
Louisiana	3	2	2	−1	−1	1
North Carolina	8	2	2	4	−5	2
Texas	11	11	8	3	−2	2
Virginia	5	4	2	1	−2	2
	27 (45%)	19 (32%)	14 (23%)	7 (9%)	−10 (−20%)	7 (11%)
OTHER STATES:						
Alabama	3	3	1	1	−2	1
Florida	15	3	5	5	−2	1
Georgia	7	1	3	6	−7	2
Maryland	4	0	4	1	−1	0
South Carolina	4	1	1	2	−3	1
	33 (60%)	8 (15%)	14 (25%)	15 (24%)	−15 (−31%)	5 (7%)
TOTAL	60 (52%)	27 (23%)	28 (24%)	22 (16%)	−25 (−25%)	12 (9%)

percentage of moderate Democratic representatives. The percentage of Democratic representatives in these states fell from 46 percent in 1990 to 25 percent in 1992 to 15 percent in 1994. White moderates lost ground even in states with Democratic gerrymanders, shrinking from 52 percent in 1990 to 42 percent in 1992 to 32 percent in 1994 of the total number of representatives.

Unfortunately for black substantive representation, liberal gains fail to account for the decline of the white moderates. Republicans gained nine additional seats in 1992 in states with new black districts. All of these Republican gains occurred in states without Democratic gerrymanders. The percentage of Republicans in these states rose from 36 to 49 percent after the election. Republicans made no gains in the four states that adopted Democratic gerrymanders—an astounding achievement on the part of Democrats, given the growth in Republican suburbs in these states during the 1980s. Gerrymanders did not successfully protect Democrats over the long term. The GOP picked up just over one-half of their thirteen seat gain in 1994 in Democratic gerrymander states.

Racial redistricting decreased black substantive representation despite the sharp increase in the number of reliable liberal votes. The total number of potential votes that any liberal policy supported by African Americans can hope to receive on the floor of the House has dropped due to the increase in the number of Republicans. As explained below in more detail, the base of support for such policies may have risen, but attracting the total votes needed for passage has become more difficult.

Racial Redistricting Caused the Democrats to Lose Seats

1992

Racial redistricting explains at least one-half of 1992 Republican gains, though the national Republican tide that gave Republicans control of the House for the first time in forty years accounts for most of the new seats won by Republicans in 1994. Kevin Hill found that the Democrats lost four seats in 1992 that they held in 1990 due to racial redistricting: the Sixth District of Alabama and the First, Third, and Fourth Districts of Georgia.[12] Racial redistricting reduced the black percentage of the population in Alabama's Sixth District from 37 to 9 percent. The black share of the population declined from 32 to 23 percent in Georgia's First District, from 35 to 18 percent in Georgia's Third District, and from 25 to 12 percent in Georgia's Fourth District. Even the NAACP Legal Defense Fund (LDF) Report, the only source that actually contends that racial redistricting resulted in a net gain of seats for the Democrats, concedes that the Democrats could have won the three Georgia seats in 1992 if racial redistricting had not occurred. The LDF Report does not discuss the effect of racial redistricting in Alabama.[13]

Racial redistricting also cost the Democrats the opportunity of picking up the open Republican Second District of Alabama. Republican Terry Everett defeated Democrat George Wallace Jr. by 3,571 votes after racial redistricting reduced the percentage of blacks in the district from 32 to 24 percent.[14] Redistricting may have cost the Democrats one more seat in 1992 by shaving the black share of Florida's Fourth District from 28 to 6 percent. Unlike in the other districts, it is not clear that racial redistricting completely accounts for the loss of this open Democratic seat. Racial redistricting minimally resulted in making the district solidly Republican instead of highly competitive for both parties. Racial redistricting thus accounts for five or six Democratic losses in 1992.

Redistricting may have cost the Democrats an additional seat in Florida. Republican Clay Shaw won reelection in 1992 from Florida's Twenty-Second District by a margin of 36,771 votes after redistricting reduced the percentage of blacks in his district from 26 to 3 percent. Former Florida Senate president Gwen Margolis, Shaw's 1992 opponent, worked to shape the district to her advantage before departing the state legislature so the district is excluded from the total count of districts lost because of racial redistricting. Margolis might have had greater success in drawing a seat for herself if she had been able to remove black voters from the adjoining Twenty-Third District, a newly created black majority district.

Racial redistricting definitely cannot account for two of the seats picked up from Democrats by Republicans in 1992. Redistricting altered South Carolina's Fourth District only marginally. Democrat Liz Patterson's defeat surprised observers less than her three victories in this heavily Republican district. Maryland Democrat Tom McMillen lost reelection after redistricting collapsed his seat and the seat held by Republican Wayne Gilchrest in a manner favorable to Gilchrest. Efforts to protect two other white incumbents, white Democrat Steny Hoyer and white Republican Helen Delich Bentley, explain the plan's configuration. McMillen could have been given a more congenial district but Democratic Governor Schaefer would not permit the legislature to collapse Bentley's district, instead of McMillen's, into Gilchrest's district because of his ties to fellow Baltimorean Bentley.

1994

Estimates of the total number of seats lost due to racial redistricting in 1994 vary more widely than for 1992 alone. Carol Swain conservatively estimates that racial redistricting cost the Democrats "no fewer than five seats in 1992 and at least twelve in 1994" for a total of seventeen seats over the two elections. David Bositis of the Joint Center for Political and Economic Studies concurs with these estimates.[15] Charles Bullock and Michael Kelly similarly contend that racial redistricting contributed to Democratic losses. Neither Bullock nor Kelly provide an exact estimate of the number of seats lost by Democrats due to racial redistricting. However, Bullock writes: "At the simplest level, the impact of redistricting is apparent when the number of black voters removed from a district exceeds the GOP victory margin."[16] Bullock's method suggests that racial redistricting explains six Democratic losses in 1992 and an additional three Democratic defeats in 1994.

Handley, Grofman, and Arden believe that racial redistricting cost the Democrats no more than ten to eleven seats and potentially as few as two to five seats.[17] Petrocik and Desposato analyzed the aggregate vote shift between 1992 and 1994 and concluded that the shift away from the Democrats by white voters, rather than racial redistricting, accounts for most Republican gains in 1994. Petrocik and Desposato correctly argue that the trend by white voters toward the Republicans accounts for most Republican gains. Their focus on the aggregate shift in voting patterns, however, prevents them from being able to answer the key question of whether a fraction of the seats gained by Republicans could have been held by Democrats if racial redistricting had not occurred. The experience of several individual Democrats could deviate from the typical Democrat who would have lost reelection that year in any case.[18]

Richard Engstrom claims that the idea that the GOP has gained seats due to redistricting is a "myth."[19] Engstrom notes that Republicans gained seats at approximately the same rate in states that did and did not create new black districts, but does not disprove the notion that Republicans might have won fewer seats in states that created new black majority districts if racial redistricting had not occurred. He examines aggregate gains in the Republican share of the vote in his discussion of individual states but does not study individual districts to see if Democrats might have won them if redistricting had not reduced the percentage of blacks in the district.

The LDF Report claims that racial redistricting prevented the Democrats from losing even more seats but it is so riddled with errors that it cannot be taken seriously. Among its numerous errors, the LDF Report underestimates changes in the racial composition of districts due to redistricting. The LDF Report derived its statistics on the percentage of African Americans and Latinos in the pre-1992 districts from the 1980 census instead of the 1990 census despite major increases in the minority share of the population between 1980 and 1990 in several of the districts affected by racial redistricting.[20] The LDF Report fails to consider that the Democratic vote would have been higher in 1994 if racial redistricting had not occurred. Whites residing in black districts voted for Democratic candidates at a lower rate than if black majority districts had not been created and the Democrats had nominated white candidates. Black candidates would regularly win election from white majority districts if whites supported black candidates in large numbers and racial redistricting would not be necessary to assure the election of more than token numbers of African Americans to the House.

None of the studies examining the effect of racial redistricting in 1994 consider that the Republican vote ballooned in part due to the incumbency advantage. Republicans benefited from the incumbency advantage in seats taken from the Democrats due to racial redistricting in 1992 in addition to highly favorable national trends. In 1994, Democrats lost the incumbency advantage picked up in 1992 by the Republicans due to racial redistricting. Gary Jacobson's estimates for the incumbency advantage make it possible to estimate what the vote totals would have been if the incumbency advantage had rested with the Democrats in 1994.[21] These estimates suggest that in 1994 incumbent Democrats could have held all of the seats that the Democrats lost in 1992 due to racial redistricting if they had not originally been lost.

Almost all analysts of the 1994 elections results agree that the Democrats would have carried North Carolina's Second and Third Districts if racial redistricting had not cut the percentage of blacks from 40 to 22 percent in the Second District and 26 to 21 percent in the Third District.[22] Retaining a greater share of his black constituents almost certainly would have allowed incumbent Martin Lancaster to overcome a 7,451 vote deficit in the Third District. Republican David Funderburk could not have amassed a 17,085 vote margin if the share of blacks in the Second District had not declined by 18 percent. Counting five seats from 1992 and these two seats in 1994, the Democrats minimally lost seven seats due to racial redistricting.

The Democrats most likely lost up to four more seats than this conservative estimate. Besides the Fourth and Twenty-Second Districts of Florida (see discussion above of losses in 1992), at least two other Democratic losses can reasonably be attributed to racial redistricting. Incumbent Democrat Herb Klein lost his bid for reelection from New Jersey's Eighth District by only 1,833 votes after redistricting reduced the district's minority population by 4 percent. Dan Rostenkowski could have easily won reelection from the Fifth District of Illinois despite his indictment if redistricting had not sliced the percentage of blacks from 10 to 1 percent and the percentage of Latinos from 42 to 13 percent.

Racial Redistricting and Public Policy

Racial redistricting has resulted in the election of a Congress less likely to enact liberal measures favored by African Americans and has greatly altered the makeup of Congress. The following analysis shows the direct effect of these changes on the aggregate roll-call voting behavior of the House of

Representatives on issues of deep concern to African Americans. Before turning to the analysis of actual issues and House roll-call votes, the methodology used to arrive at these conclusions will be described in detail. Readers interested in getting to the results quickly can skip this section.

Using the Poole-Rosenthal Scores to Predict
Roll-Call Votes

The Poole-Rosenthal scores can be used for much more than merely ranking the relative liberalism or conservatism of members of Congress. The scores provide the best means of predicting how various individual or groups of members will vote on the floor of the House on any given issue. The scores further allow prediction of how representatives would have voted on measures that came before the House in different legislative sessions, since they are comparable across Congresses. This stability makes it possible to examine a roll-call vote from the 102nd Congress, elected in 1990 prior to redistricting, and estimate how the 103rd Congress, elected in 1992 after redistricting, would have voted on the same issue. Conversely, using the same technique, one can determine how members of the 102nd Congress would have voted on issues before the 103rd Congress.

A simple example demonstrates how the Poole-Rosenthal scores allow for the estimation of changes in support for legislation across different years. Suppose that the legislature contains just five members, called A, B, C, D, and E, with Poole-Rosenthal scores of −.5, −.3, −.1, .2, and .4. As shown in section a of figure 6.3, the legislators can be arrayed along a number line according to their scores. The probability of any legislator voting with the conservatives on any given issue rises as their Poole-Rosenthal score becomes more positive, so E is much more likely than the other legislators to vote conservative. The legislators and the number line can be divided into two groups based on how they voted on an issue. For example, as shown in section b of figure 6.3, on a vote to increase the minimum wage, A, B, and C might vote yea, while D and E vote nay. The bill would pass by a 3–2 margin. The division between the yeas and nays determines the position of the "cutting line" on this issue. For the minimum wage vote, the cutting line falls around 0.

Knowing the position of the cutting line on an issue makes it possible to determine how differently constituted legislatures might have voted on the same issue. Suppose an election occurs and five new legislators, P, Q, R, S, and T, with Poole-Rosenthal scores of −.4, −.2, .1, .3, and .5 win election (see sec. c of figure 6.3). Based upon the knowledge from the previous legislature that cutting line for the minimum wage bill falls at 0, one can predict that if the bill comes before the new legislature, P and Q will probably vote yea while R, S, and T will mostly likely vote nay. Unlike in the first legislature,

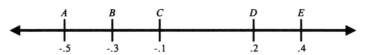

(a) Legislature 1

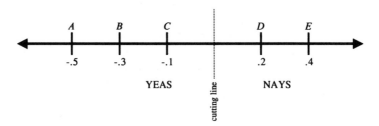

(b) Legislature 1: Minimum Wage Vote Passes 3–2

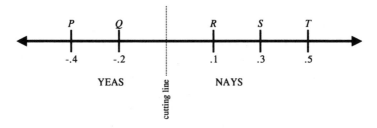

(c) Legislature 2: Same Vote in New Legislature Fails 3–2

6.3. Application of the Poole-Rosenthal Scores to a Hypothetical Legislature.

the bill would fail by a 3–2 margin. The probability of making an error in prediction increases the closer the position of a legislator to the cutting line because swing votes are harder to predict.

The effect of racial redistricting on public policy votes in Congress may be estimated using the same techniques. Examining actual votes, the position of the cutting line may be determined for a wide assortment of votes in any two Congresses. Once the position of the cutting line has been found utilizing the real roll-call votes from one Congress, it is possible to predict how the other Congress would have voted on the same issue.

Racial Redistricting Changes Roll-Call Vote Outcomes
to the Detriment of Black Interests

The change in representation in states with new black districts depends on the ideological content of the vote and whether or not the state adopted a Democratic gerrymander (see fig. 6.4). Ideology matters because racial redistricting does not change roll-call vote outcomes by moving all representatives marginally to the Right or to the Left. Racial redistricting resulted in the election of more staunch liberal Democrats and conservative Republicans at the expense of centrist white Democrats. Racial redistricting consequently does not result in a uniform swing on roll-call votes regardless of where the roll-call falls on the liberal-conservative spectrum.

Racial redistricting resulted in the election of congressional delegations more likely to cast more liberal votes in states with Democratic gerrymanders for almost all votes. Representatives from Democratic gerrymander states cast more conservative votes due to racial redistricting only on extremely liberal votes with Poole-Rosenthal cutting lines of less than −.4. Liberals already lose these votes by such large margins that this small conservative shift (only two votes) could not possibly change the outcome of any roll-call votes. Racial redistricting advanced both descriptive and substantive representation of African Americans in Democratic gerrymander states.

The link between the ideology of the vote and the change in the outcome due to racial redistricting differs radically in states that did not adopt Democratic gerrymanders. The predicted shift in the outcome of the roll-call vote in these states depends heavily on the ideological content of the vote. Liberals gain as many as eleven additional votes on mainstream liberal legislation with Poole-Rosenthal scores ranging from −.33 to −.08. Racial redistricting also increased the size of the lopsided liberal majority on highly conservative issues with Poole-Rosenthal scores greater than .40. Conservatives made strong gains on moderate and mainstream conservative legislation with Poole-Rosenthal scores between −.07 and .36 in states that did gerrymander in favor of the Democrats. Liberals lost more than five votes on almost all of these votes and and over ten votes on most roll-call votes with scores ranging from −.02 to .27. Conservatives also made noticeable gains on highly liberal roll-call votes that have no chance of passage.

The relationship between roll-call vote ideology and racial redistricting strongly advantages conservatives. Legislation that will attract a majority of the House lies in an ideological range in which conservatives gained votes thanks to racial redistricting. African Americans picked up support through redistricting only on votes for liberal causes that will probably not pass Congress soon no matter the redistricting plan. Racial redistricting effectively raised the base of support for liberal measures in the/ House but did not bring them closer to passage. Racial redistricting actually endangered liberal

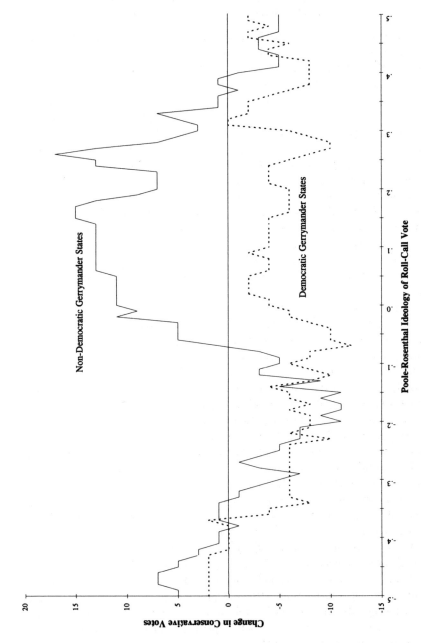

6.4. Predicted Change in Roll-Call Votes in States with New Black Majority Districts, 1991–1993.

initiatives with a real chance of passage on the floor of the House by moving the center of the House in a more conservative direction.

Democratic gerrymanders mitigate the negative impact of racial redistricting in other states with new black districts. The Supreme Court, however, has been extremely critical in several decisions of the tortured lines required both to draw new black districts and to protect white Democrats. Bizarre boundaries serve as prima facie evidence of racial gerrymandering that a narrow majority of the Supreme Court finds unconstitutional. In *Miller v. Johnson* and *Bush v. Vera*, the Supreme Court upheld lower court rulings striking down districts in Georgia and Texas. On the same day as it handed down its decision in the Texas case, the Court declared in *Shaw v. Hunt* that the Twelfth District of North Carolina is an unconstitutional racial gerrymander. All of the Democratic gerrymander states contain black majority districts with boundaries more erose than in the Georgia case and are consequently vulnerable to legal challenge.

The overall direction is clear: the Court plans to constrain the use of creative cartography to draw additional black districts. The negative impact of racial redistricting on black substantive representation will likely increase as the judiciary overturns or states repeal plans that fail to meet its guidelines. African Americans will suffer a drop in descriptive representation as plans contain fewer black districts or a more severe decline in substantive representation as states redraw these districts more compactly.

Conclusion

Efforts to maximize the number of black elected members of the House and pro-black congressional legislation work at cross-purposes. Republicans usually benefit from racial redistricting, since creating new majority black districts inevitably concentrates Democrats in a few districts. Republican gains undermine attempts by representatives to win passage of legislation supported by African Americans. Serious efforts to boost black substantive representation through the creation of safe Democratic seats would destroy existing black majority districts and likely reduce the number of black representatives. Black and white Democrats can work together to enact redistricting plans that minimize the conflict between these two goals. Packing Republicans into a few districts and not making new black majority districts more than 55 percent black minimizes the threat to white incumbent Democrats and black substantive representation. These plans invariably require extremely creative line drawing. As chapter 7 explains, the Supreme Court's decisions in *Miller v. Johnson*, *Bush v. Vera*, and *Shaw v. Hunt* makes it unlikely that these plans will withstand legal challenge.

7

THE OUTLOOK FOR THE FUTURE

FEW BLACKS and no Latinos sat in the Congress at the time of the passage of the Voting Rights Act of 1965. Thirty-eight African Americans and seventeen Latinos won election to the 103rd Congress in 1992 after more than a generation of fighting to expand minority political opportunities through the creation of majority-minority districts. Racial redistricting under the aegis of the Voting Rights Act explains these impressive gains. African Americans and Latinos find it extremely difficult to win election to the House of Representatives from majority white districts despite victories by a few high-profile minority candidates. The civil rights movement eliminated virtually all legal barriers to minority participation in the political process, but attitudes often change more slowly than laws. The racial composition of a district remains centrally important to the exclusion of all other factors in determining the race of its representative several decades after the passage of the Voting Rights Act.

States did not immediately rush to draw new majority-minority congressional districts upon passage of the act in 1965. Civil rights advocates fought for over twenty years to gain acceptance for a broad interpretation of voting rights that went beyond the simple ability to cast a ballot without hindrance. Proponents of racial redistricting gradually won the right to file suit against redistricting plans that diluted black and Latino voting strength under Section 2 of the act. The Justice Department gained the power to block redistricting plans that diluted minority votes under Section 5 of the act. States drew numerous new majority-minority districts during the 1990 redistricting cycle in an effort to protect their redistricting plans against both federal and judicial action. African Americans and Latinos continue to compose a greater percentage of the population than of the House despite the substantial increase in the number of majority-minority districts and minority representatives in the 103rd Congress.

Just as opponents of racial redistricting inaccurately characterize majority-minority districts as unnecessary to the election of more than token numbers of African Americans and Latinos to the House of Representatives, supporters overestimate the proportion of blacks and Latinos needed to guarantee the election of a minority representative. Relatively low registration and turnout rates and a comparatively young minority population make it more difficult for blacks and Latinos to win election. The so-called 65 percent rule supported by many racial redistricting advocates nevertheless severely overestimates the percentage of blacks or Latinos required to assure the election of a minority representative. Fifty-five percent black districts will elect African Americans to the House in most parts of the country. Most 55 percent Latino districts will send a Latino representative to Washington. The presence of Latinos reduces the percentage of blacks needed to assure the election of a black representative. Raising the percentage of citizens in a district correspondingly lowers the percentage of Latinos required to assure the election of a Latino representative. Latinos will find it easier to win election to the House than African Americans as Latino citizenship rates rise.

The seniority system, which greatly aided the efforts of entrenched white supremacists to block minority political equality, now lends its power to the growing contingent of black and Latino legislators. African-American and Mexican-American members chaired a wide variety of House committees until the Republicans won control of the House in 1994. Puerto Rican and Cuban-American legislators, still small in numbers, have yet to occupy any influential committee chairs. Aside from the few Republican minority legislators, mostly Cuban, black and Latino legislators greatly benefited from Democratic control of the House. African-American and Latino representatives accrued over time the power temporarily lost to minority communities when new black and Latino representatives replaced senior white incumbents.

Determining the effect of racial redistricting on the substantive representation of minority interests is far more complicated than outlining the solid link between race and minority descriptive representation. Representatives become noticeably more responsive to their African-American constituents once a district reaches 40 percent black. African-American residents of 40 to 50 percent black influence districts cannot necessarily elect a black representative, but blacks in coalition with either Latinos or white liberals can prevent the election of a conservative opposed to their policy goals. The composition of the nonblack portion of the population largely determines the race of the representative. Whites almost invariably represent black influence districts with white majorities. African Americans usually represent districts with majority-minority populations.

Raising the black population, even within majority white districts, increases the responsiveness of all representatives except northern Democrats to African-American interests. This responsiveness marks a major departure from the link between race and representation prior to the Voting Rights Act. In his landmark study of southern politics prior to the Voting Rights Act, V.O. Key found that representatives actually became more conservative as the black population rose. The key difference between the pre– and post–Voting Rights Act eras is that southern blacks can vote. Pre-Voting Rights Act representatives responded only to the interests of their white constituents. Whites in areas with large numbers of blacks supported white supremacy with particular fervor and their representatives reflected their views. Members of Congress now face reelection in a racially mixed electorate. Many southern Democrats depend upon biracial coalitions to gain reelection. Blacks successfully exert influence over their members of Congress despite the winner-take-all system of elections.

Regional differences in the ideology of whites and the dispersion of blacks explain regional disparities in responsiveness to changes in the share of the black population. The seeming lack of responsiveness by northern Democrats to changes in the black population reflects that most central city representatives support policies favored by blacks regardless of the size of the black population. Demographics force mapmakers to draw compact black majority districts in central cities in the North. Fortuitously for African Amerians and Democrats, the most liberal nonblack populations in America live in close proximity to these districts. Latinos and Jews continue to vote strongly Democratic despite declines in Democratic voting among other nonblack groups. Catholics vote more Republican than Latino or Jewish Americans but still cast a majority of their votes for Democratic congressional candidates. Most central city districts elect liberal Democrats no matter how the redistricting plan slices the city into districts. Drawing new black districts removes African Americans from surrounding districts but other liberal whites usually replace them. Varying the black population above or below the 40 percent threshold consequently has little impact on black substantive representation in the North. Racial redistricting usually increases the number of minority elected officials without harming either overall Democratic prospects or black substantive representation in either individual districts or delegations taken as a whole.

Racial redistricting has disastrous implications for black substantive representation in the South unless Democrats successfully manage to win the adoption of a partisan gerrymander. Racial polarization forces white southern representatives to pay close attention to the racial balance of their districts. Drawing new black districts in the South often requires connecting central city and rural black populations. Relatively few Jews or Latinos live in the South outside of Florida and Texas. The South contains disproportionate numbers of white Protestants and white born-again Christians who vote overwhelmingly Republican in congressional elections. Concentrating blacks in these districts increases the conservatism of surrounding districts because of the absence of large populations of nonblack liberals in most parts of the South. Democratic representatives from districts with smaller white populations must adopt more conservative policy stances or risk alienating the enlarged white majority and losing reelection. Some districts change enough racially and ideologically to elect Republicans in place of Democrats.

Democrats attempted to mitigate the negative effects of racial redistricting on their party in Louisiana, North Carolina, Texas, and Virginia through partisan gerrymandering. Packing white Republican voters into a few districts boosts Democratic prospects just as packing Democrats into a few districts aids Republicans. Strategic Democratic mapmakers limit the number of black Democrats in new black majority districts to around 55 percent black, just enough to assure the election of an African-American representative. This policy maximizes the efficiency of the Democratic vote by packing Republicans and minimizing the concentration of African Americans. Democratic ingenuity in drafting redistricting plans permitted the enhancement of black substantive representation in some states despite racial redistricting. Most substantive representation gains resulted from Democratic gerrymanders rather than from the creation of new majority-minority districts.

This marginal positive effect of racial redistricting in Democratic gerrymander states fails to outweigh the deleterious effect of racial redistricting on black substantive representation in states without Democratic gerrymanders. Republican gains due to the decimation of white moderates in all states with new black districts more than compensate for gains made by Democrats in Democratic gerrymander states. Republicans conservatively won at least six more seats in 1992 and three more seats in 1994 thanks to racial redistricting. Racial redistricting increased the contingent of House liberals but also swelled the ranks of their opponents and made the House less likely to adopt policies favored by African Americans.

Structures within Congress might mitigate the negative effect of racial redistricting on African-American substantive representation. Racial redistricting raises the number of black and Latino liberals at the expense of white moderates. Minority representatives might wield greater influence within the Democratic Caucus and successfully push the Democrats to enact liberal legislation favored by African Americans. The reduction in the number of Democrats, however, made each Democratic vote all the more crucial to the ability of the Democrats to control the House and pass legislation in the 103rd Congress. White moderates found themselves in a position to make even greater demands on the Democratic Caucus despite the reduction of their numbers. Liberals played almost no role in crafting legislation during the Republican-controlled 104th Congress.

African-American and Latino members of Congress may benefit more from the seniority system than white legislators and gain additional power. Minority legislators tend to win reelection at higher rates because they invariably win election from safe seats. Majority white constituencies rarely elect minorities, so few black and Latino representatives retire from the House to run for either governor or senator. Minority legislators may remain in the House for longer periods and accrue more seniority than their white colleagues. African Americans and Latinos should eventually chair a dispro-portionate number of congressional committees and gain enhanced power over the flow of legislation as a result. Republican control of the House ren-dered the seniority of African-American and Latino Democrats moot. Racial redistricting paradoxically worked to vastly undercut the influence of minor-ity representatives by contributing to the election of greater numbers of Re-publicans as well as minorities.

The ultimate control of the Democratic Caucus and the entire House over legislation severely constrains the ability of minority chairs to shape legisla-tion even if the Democrats should regain majority status. The Democratic Caucus can depose committee chairs who demonstrate a lack of responsive-ness to the caucus as a whole. The election of greater numbers of minorities and fewer white moderates makes this outcome less likely. More impor-tantly, committee chairs face enormous pressure to produce legislation ac-ceptable to the House as a whole. Committees that fail to craft legislation that can gain support within the House risk having their decisions over-turned by the full House. Committee chairs look foolish and weak when this happens, so they try to avoid producing legislation unnacceptable to a ma-jority of the House.

Implications of Recent Court Cases

The Supreme Court has grappled with the complex trade-offs involved in ra-cial redistricting in recent terms. A fragile five-justice majority of the Court expressed strong disapproval in *Shaw v. Reno (Shaw I)* of plans like the one in North Carolina that ignore traditional districting requirements such as compactness in an effort to draw new black districts. Justice Sandra Day O'Connor wrote:

> [W]e believe that reapportionment is one area in which appearances do matter. A reapportionment plan that includes in one district individuals who belong to the same race, but who are otherwise widely separated by geographical bound-aries, and who have little in common but the color of their skin, bears an uncomfortable reference to political apartheid.[1]

The Supreme Court did not declare the North Carolina plan unconstitu-tional in *Shaw v. Reno* despite Justice O'Connor's stinging criticisms of racial gerrymandering. The Court instead ruled that the claim of racial gerrymandering is justiciable under the Equal Protection Clause of the Constitution and remanded the case back to the district court with orders that "If the allegation of racial gerrymandering remains uncontradicted, the District Court must determine whether the North Carolina plan is narrowly tailored to further a compelling governmental interest."

The Supreme Court's opinion in *Shaw v. Reno* was sufficiently vague that district courts around the South interpreted its meaning in widely different and contradictory ways. The lower courts vociferously argued over the standard of proof for racial gerrymandering and the meaning of the "narrowly tailored to further a compelling governmental interest" standard invoked by *Shaw I.*

The District Court for the Southern District of Georgia extended the Supreme Court's attack on racial redistricting by lowering the threshold for a finding of racial gerrymandering. Georgia's Eleventh District stretched from Atlanta to Savannah to Augusta to Macon to gather black voters, but its boundaries are no less compact than many mostly white districts around the country.[2] The Court's decision striking down the Eleventh District in *Johnson v. Miller* effectively placed a heavier burden on states creating new majority-minority districts than on states drawing oddly shaped districts for other reasons.

The Supreme Court largely upheld this decision on appeal and dealt a major setback to proponents of racial redistricting. The Supreme Court's 5–4 majority ruled in *Miller v. Johnson* that utilizing race as the "predominant factor" in redistricting violates the Equal Protection Clause of the Constitution. In striking down the boundaries of Georgia's Eleventh District, the Court rejected the argument that the state had a compelling interest in drawing a third black majority district to receive preclearance under Section 5 of the Voting Rights Act. The Justice Department overstepped its authority and the Constitution by pressing Georgia to create a third black majority district, according to the Court's majority. States cannot use the Voting Rights Act as a justification for racial gerrymandering or as a shield against constitutional challenges to redistricting plans. The decision severely undercuts the ability of the Justice Department to use its review powers under Section 5 of the Voting Rights Act to force states to create new majority-minority districts.[3]

The *Miller* decision encouraged attacks on majority-minority districts and placed states in a very difficult position. Working to achieve preclearance under Section 5 or to avoid a lawsuit under Section 2 of the Voting Rights Act may provide evidence that race was the "predominant factor" in redistricting. Virtually all of the new majority-minority districts drawn during the 1990 redistricting cycle were created due to the pressure provided by the Voting Rights Act. Computers used in redistricting often showed the racial composition of districts as mapmakers altered district lines. As Frank Parker explained succinctly: "None of these districts was drawn accidentally."[4]

The Court indicated in *Miller* that it was suspicious of defenses of majority-minority districts as political, rather than racial, gerrymanders. Georgia could have drawn more compact districts if legislators had paid less attention to nonracial political considerations. Justice Ginsburg explained in her dissenting opinion in *Miller* that efforts to accommodate the wishes of various state legislators contributed substantially to the odd shape of the Eleventh District.[5] The Court's majority nevertheless ruled that the district violates the Equal Protection Clause because race was the predominant factor in its creation even if its erose boundaries result largely from politics, rather than being necessary to concentrate minority voters. *Shaw v. Reno* focused on bizarre district boundaries, but *Miller* stated that the district's shape serves only as circumstantial evidence of a racial gerrymander, and does not constitute a constitutional violation itself.

The majority opinion, written by Justice Kennedy, did not distinguish between districting plans intended to benefit minority voters and plans designed to limit their opportunities to gain descriptive representation. Justice Stevens wrote in his dissent: "Equally distressing is the Court's equation of traditional gerrymanders, designed to maintain or enhance a dominant group's power, with a dominant group's decision to share its power with a previously underrepresented group."[6] Justice Stevens further argued that the majority opinion rested on an internal contradiction. The Court decries racial redistricting because it assumes that "individuals of the same race share a single political interest."[7] Justice Stevens contended in his dissent that the white plaintiffs cannot have suffered any representational harms if blacks do not vote cohesively and substantially differently than whites as a group, so they have no standing to bring suit. Finding that the white plaintiffs have suffered harms depends upon the assumption that plaintiffs have different political interests than the black residents of the district.[8] The Court ignored overwhelming evidence of racial polarization in its effort to avoid racially stereotyping individual voters. Ominously for minority representation, groups of voters, rather than individuals, elect representatives.

Miller v. Johnson provides a brake on efforts to maximize the number of majority-minority districts but does not permit states to undercut minority descriptive representation by intentionally dismantling compact districts with large numbers of minority voters. The majority opinion emphatically restated the "no retrogression" standard outlined in *Beer v. United States* at the same time as it struck down Georgia's Eleventh District. The Court tried to achieve a balance of sorts by reiterating its opposition to vote dilution as well as egregious racial gerrymanders.[9]

The Supreme Court gave a more concrete indication that it will permit some racial redistricting when it dismissed a challenge to California's congressional district map only hours after issuing its decision in *Miller v. Johnson*.[10] California's districts are more compact than the Democratic gerrymander in place during the 1980s and have far less tortured boundaries than most new majority-minority districts in other parts of the nation. Many of California's districts contain a diverse melange of blacks, Latinos, Asians, and whites. The special panel that drew California's districts apparently made less effort than mapmakers in other states to separate minorities from whites or each other even as they preserved and created several new Latino and mixed majority-minority districts. Some of the diversity within California's districts results from California's demographics. It would have been quite difficult to draw districts giving any one group a majority in some areas. Mapmakers in other states managed to give dominance to one group in equally diverse areas, so California could have conceivably contrived a plan to accomplish the same goal.

Cases on many redistricting plans, including the Georgia plan, continued to wend their way through the judicial system after the *Miller* decision. The District Court for the Eastern District of North Carolina upheld the redistricting plan that originally provoked the Supreme Court's ire in *Shaw v. Reno* on remand as *Shaw v. Hunt*. The district court deemed North Carolina's plan a racial gerrymander in line with the Supreme Court's ringing denunciations of the plan as a form of "political apartheid" in *Shaw I*. The district court surprisingly found that the redistricting plan furthers the state's "compelling governmental interest" in complying with Sections 2 and 5 of the Voting Rights Act and creating separate urban and rural black majority districts. The court concluded that the plan was "narrowly tailored" to serve these governmental interests. The two new black majority districts in North Carolina have slim African-American voting majorities that provide black voters a reasonable chance of electing representatives of their choice. Although the districts are bizarrely shaped, they are "highly homogeneous in terms of their citizens' material conditions and interests and do not significantly inhibit access to and responsiveness of their elected representatives."[11]

One month after the district court upheld the North Carolina plan in *Shaw v. Hunt*, a district court in Texas overturned several of that state's districts as racial gerrymanders in *Vera v. Richards*. In its opinion, the District Court for the Southern District of Texas harshly criticized the majority's opinion in *Shaw v. Hunt* as improperly interpreting the Supreme Court's intentions in *Shaw v. Reno*. The majority wrote: "With due respect to the two-judge majority on remand of Shaw, we disagree strongly that the misshapen boundaries of a racially constructed district are merely prima facie evidence of a constitutional violation and not part of its essence." The district court further made clear that it viewed incumbent protection as insufficient to justify the adoption of a racial gerrymander.[12]

The sharp disagreement among the district courts as well as within the Supreme Court led to the Supreme Court sensibly granting certiorari in both the North Carolina and Texas cases. The Supreme Court essentially sided with the Texas court in its decisions in *Bush v. Vera* and *Shaw v. Hunt (Shaw II)*. Justice O'Connor cited the submission by Texas to the Justice Department for preclearance under Section 5 as proof of the legislature's racial motivations in her opinion for the majority in *Bush v. Vera*. The Court remained extremely divided in these two 5–4 decisions, with several justices writing concurring or dissenting opinions. Justice O'Connor even wrote a concurring opinion to her own majority opinion in *Bush v. Vera*.

The decisions in these cases clarified some questions surrounding racial redistricting but left others unsettled. In the context of the North Carolina case, the Court made clear that states could not address potential Section 2 violations in one part of the state by drawing a majority-minority district in another part. The creation of North Carolina's elongated Twelfth District, an urban district in the central Piedmont section of the state, resulted directly from the Justice Department's Section 5 objection to the state's original plan on the grounds that North Carolina could have drawn a majority black and Lumbee Indian district in the rural southeastern part of the state. The Twelfth District did not include minorities residing in this part of the state so it did not address any potential violation of Section 2, according to the Court's majority. At the same time, the Court left open the question of whether the attorney general even has the right to deny preclearance under Section 5 to plans that may contain Section 2 violations.

Bush v. Vera and *Shaw v. Hunt* provided somewhat clearer direction to states about when they may create majority-minority districts. Complying with the Voting Rights Act, as interpreted by the Court, can serve as a "compelling" state interest for racial redistricting. States may intentionally create new majority-minority districts if the districts prevent the state from committing a violation of Section 2, according to the three-prong test outlined by the Court in *Thornburg v. Gingles*. The Court decided in *Gingles* that failure to draw a majority-minority district violates Section 2 if the minority group is: (1) "sufficiently large and geographically compact to constitute a majority in a single-member district," (2) "politically cohesive," and (3) usually unable to elect its preferred candidate due to racial bloc voting.[13] Neither *Bush v. Vera* or *Shaw v. Hunt*, however, details the latitude that states have in constructing new districts that meet these criteria. The dissenters in *Bush* and *Shaw II* contend that the decisions will force states to guess the district that the courts would have imposed if the state had lost a Section 2 suit challenging their redistricting plan. They believe that the decision invites litigation by people unhappy with the redistricting plan who claim that a more compact majority-minority district could have been drawn. Racial bloc voting may also make it nearly impossible for judges to sort out whether lines were drawn for political or racial reasons. Justice Souter fears that courts will end up judging "beauty contests" of competing redistricting plans.

The divided nature of the Court suggests that the interpretation of the Voting Rights Act could shift sharply again if the composition of the Court changes. None of the decisions attacking racial redistricting attracted more than a 5–4 majority of the Court. The dissenters have repeatedly expressed their desire and willingness to overturn the precedents set in *Shaw I and II*, *Miller*, and *Bush*. Several of the justices in the majority believe that the current attack on racial redistricting does not go far enough. They believe that utilizing race in drawing districts invokes strict scrutiny as to whether or not race was the "predominant factor" in drawing district lines. The next retirements and appointments to the Supreme Court will play a major role in shaping the Court's interpretation of the Voting Rights Act and the Equal Protection Clause.

In the meantime, the question of exactly how many majority-minority districts will be erased lies in the hands of Justice O'Connor—the key voter in all of the redistricting cases. Justice O'Connor hinted in a two-paragraph concurring opinion in *Miller* that she was less inclined than her brethren in the majority to eliminate majority-minority districts:

> Application of the Court's standard does not throw into doubt the vast majority of the Nation's 435 congressional districts, where presumably the States have drawn the boundaries in accordance with their customary districting principles. That is so even though race may well have been considered in the redistricting process.[14]

Justice O'Connor's statement in *Miller* has turned out to be largely wishful thinking. The Supreme Court's decisions attacking racial redistricting have already begun to reshape redistricting plans around the nation at all levels of government.

The Court's decisions have directly required redrawing plans in Georgia, North Carolina, and Texas. The Georgia legislature could not agree on a new plan after the decision in *Miller*, so the district court in Georgia imposed a new plan for the 1996 elections. The court eliminated not only the Eleventh District at issue in *Miller* but also reduced the percentage of voting-age blacks in the Second District, represented by African-American Sanford Bishop, from 52 to 35 percent. The decision to eliminate the Second District is currently on appeal. The district court in North Carolina decided to allow the 1996 elections to proceed under the existing district lines and to require that the legislature enact new districts by April 1997. The district court in Texas once again departed from the path followed by the court in North Carolina and redrew the district lines even though Texas had already held its congressional primaries. The Texas plan changed the boundaries of thirteen of the state's thirty districts. The plan eliminated no majority-minority districts but they are more compact and contain a greater mixture of Latinos and African Americans.[15]

Plans in other states have been challenged in court or altered in an attempt to avoid lawsuits. The District Court for the Western District of Louisiana became the first lower court to apply the decision in *Shaw I* in *Hays v. Louisiana (Hays I)*. This lengthy challenge to Louisiana's congressional redistricting plan focused on the Fourth District of Louisiana. Nick-named the "Zorro district," the Fourth District meandered all over the state in a rough Z shape as it collected black voters from every major town outside of New Orleans, as well as from rural areas. In striking down Louisiana's congressional redistricting plan, the court harshly criticized the Fourth District as an example of the worst type of racial gerrymandering. Anticipating the Supreme Court's later decisions, the court declared that Louisiana does not have the right to draw a second black district either of its own volition or because it is compelled to by the Justice Department unless it is feasible to draw a compact district.[16] The district court specifically attacked the U.S. Attorney General's Office for requiring that Louisiana create a second black majority district and going beyond the "no retrogression" principle enunciated in *Beer v. United States.*

Louisiana redrew its congressional district boundaries after the Court's ruling to make the Fourth District substantially more compact, though the new boundaries still cut across many parish boundaries. The new boundaries reduced the black percentage of the Fourth District from 67 to 59 percent black. Louisiana's reworked Fourth District followed the Red River and was not as misshapen as the original version, but it still cut across many parish lines in an effort to collect enough African-American voters to form a majority. The district court vitiated this new redistricting plan as yet another racial gerrymander. The court then imposed its own plan, which eliminated Louisiana's second black majority district in favor of creating more compact districts that violated few parish boundaries.[17] The Supreme Court then vacated the district court's decision because the plaintiffs lacked standing in *U.S. v. Hays (Hays II)*. The plaintiffs did not reside in the redrawn black majority Fourth District, so the Supreme Court ruled that they had not personally "been subjected to racial classification" and suffered any harms that entitled them to sue.[18] New plaintiffs filed suit and the district court overturned Louisiana's plan for a third time in early 1996.[19]

Florida redrew five districts in the northeastern part of the state after a district court ruled the Third District an unconstitutional racial gerrymander. The new plan reduced the black share of the Third District's voting-age population to 42 percent. The district court agreed to let the new plan stand for the 1996 elections but decided to issue its final decision on the plan after the elections. The revised Third District is more compact but still extends from Jacksonville to Orlando. Florida contains several other districts that cannot hope to survive strict scrutiny. The Seventeenth District connects a thin strip of black communities in Dade County in a manner that strains the definition of contiguity as it avoids surrounding Latino areas. Redistricting afficiandos nicknamed the neighboring Latino majority Eighteenth District the "condom" district because of the way it surrounds the Seventeenth District. The Twenty-Third District strings together an exceedingly narrow band of territory running from Palm Beach County through Broward County to Dade County that contains mostly black voters. Only the compact Latino majority Twenty-First District can probably survive strict scrutiny under the *Miller* test.

Courts will inevitably strike down the Fourth District of Illinois because its bizarre shape provides ample evidence of a racial gerrymander. Popularly known as the "earmuff" district, the Fourth District connects two concentrations of Latinos in Chicago by a thin line around the neighboring black majority Seventh District. The Third District of Virginia connects black communities in Richmond, Newport News, Norfolk, and the Tidewater counties in a manner that only a desire to create a black majority district can possibly explain.

Several of the majority-minority districts in the New York City area cannot hope to pass the *Miller* test. The Twelfth District snakes around Brooklyn, Queens, and Manhattan collecting Latino voters. The mixed majority-minority Seventeenth District, currently not represented by a minority, has a compact core in the north Bronx but shoots out spurs into Westchester and the south Bronx. Most of the other truly oddly shaped districts in the New York City area (the Fifth, Seventh, Eighth, Ninth, and Eighteenth Districts) are actually white majority districts. Reconfiguring the districts so that race does not appear to be the "predominant factor" will require substantially altering the boundaries of many area districts.

Judges in Alabama and South Carolina may declare various congressional districts unlawful as well. The black majority districts in Alabama and South Carolina are not as misshapen as the North Carolina districts, but they are at least as strangely configured as the district struck down in Georgia in *Miller v. Johnson.* Race was clearly the predominant factor in drawing both Alabama's Seventh District and South Carolina's Sixth District. Both districts connect black population concentrations in distant urban centers via rural counties with black populations just like the Eleventh District of Georgia. No credible rationale besides race explains why the court that drew South Carolina's plan connected the black populations of Columbia and Charleston with rural counties that contain the highest concentrations of blacks in the state. The court that imposed Alabama's districts made race the predominant factor when it linked African Americans in Birmingham and Montgomery with lightly populated rural counties with sizable black populations.

Republicans fear and Democrats hope that distributing African Americans more evenly across districts will aid Democratic efforts to regain control of the House.[20] The partisan impact of eliminating some majority-minority districts and redrawing others more compactly will vary from state to state. Disrupting the Democratic gerrymander by redrawing majority-minority districts more compactly will most likely aid Republicans in Texas.

The new Georgia plan makes it easier for Democrats to reduce the 8–3 advantage held by the Republicans in the state's congressional delegation after the 1994 elections.[21] The total partisan effect will remain unknown until after the redrawing of the district boundaries and the conclusion of the inevitable litigation surrounding these cases. Some states will conclude redistricting for the 1990s just in time to begin redistricting for the 2000s.

Creating new majority-minority districts for a term or two may prove worse than never having drawn them at all. Racial redistricting aided Republicans in winning new seats and attracting new white voters around the South. These Republicans may be difficult to dislodge as incumbents even under changed district boundaries. The incumbency advantage may also help African-American and Latino representatives retain their seats in districts less congenial to the election of minorities, but African-American and Latino candidates have had little success winning open seats in majority white constituencies. America's temporary experiment with maximizing the number of majority-minority districts may have been disastrous for minority representation. Reducing the number of majority-minority districts will most likely undercut minority descriptive representation. African Americans will make few gains in substantive representation as even fewer black representatives win election if many of the Republicans elected thanks to racial redistricting retain their seats. African Americans and Latinos may find themselves shut out of the policy-making process in Congress to a greater extent than before racial redistricting increased the number of African-American and Latino representatives in 1992.

The conflict between descriptive and substantive representation places the black community in a dilemma. *Miller v. Johnson* forecloses the possibility of enacting Democratic gerrymanders that help minimize the conflict between these two laudable goals. Total abandonment of racial redistricting would eventually decimate the number of minority representatives elected to the House. Alabama, Florida, North Carolina, South Carolina, and Virginia all elected their first black representatives since Reconstruction in 1992 thanks to racial redistricting. The elimination of all of these districts, a very real possibility under the new *Miller* standard, would deprive African Americans of long-overdue descriptive representation. The electoral system and the legislature may gradually lose legitimacy if racial minorities can never elect a single member of their own group. The fundamental claim of any democratic electoral system to transmit the interests of all citizens to a legislature representative of all the people seems hollow in a legislature continually lacking more than token black or Latino descriptive representation.

Exclusive concentration on descriptive representation runs the risk of ignoring the negative effect of racial redistricting on substantive representation. The legislature will lose even more legitimacy if minority representatives have no impact on public policy because the white majority feels no need to pay attention to minority interests. Depriving white representatives of all of their black and Latino constituents through racial redistricting has been an excellent recipe for this type of apathy, and often outright hostility, by the majority toward the minority. Racial redistricting directly contributed to the election of greater numbers of Republicans and to the virtually irrelevant status of the Congressional Black Caucus.

Balancing the laudable goals of promoting both descriptive and substantive representation requires drawing some majority-minority districts. Prudent mapmakers with these goals in mind should consider refraining from drawing the maximum number of theoretically possible majority-minority districts. Redistricters should definitely avoid concentrating minorities in the majority-minority districts to a greater extent than necessary to guarantee the election of a minority to the House. Fifty-five percent black districts will elect an African American to the House in most parts of the country. Fifty-five percent Latino districts will most likely send Latino representatives to Washington except in areas with particularly low levels of Latino citizenship. Preventing packing allows minorities to exert influence in surrounding districts. Creating fewer majority-minority districts permits the creation of additional minority influence districts in which minorities constitute greater than 40 percent, but not a majority, of the population. African Americans exert a great deal of substantive influence in black influence districts. These districts also provide the best opportunity for blacks and Latinos to gain election from majority white districts.

No compromise between descriptive and substantive representation will satisfy everyone. The inherent conflict between descriptive and substantive representation signifies that minorities will be forced to make tough decisions about how they wish to pursue greater representation. African Americans may decide that it is worth sacrificing some substantive representation in order to gain additional descriptive representation. African Americans may think twice before continuing to pursue the maximization strategy in the face of Republican congressional gains in 1994 and strong judicial opposition. This study hopefully contributes to the debate over racial redistricting by providing a means for everyone concerned to make more informed choices about the future of minority representation in America.

NOTES

CHAPTER 1

1. Bernard Grofman, Lisa Handley, and Richard G. Niemi, *Minority Representation and the Quest for Voting Equality* (New York: Cambridge University Press, 1992), 16–19.

2. Grofman, Handley, and Niemi, 23–26.

3. *Allen v. State Board of Elections*, 393 U.S. 544 (1969), 831–833.

4. *Miller v. Johnson*, 1995 U.S. Lexis 4462.

5. Lani Guinier, *The Tyranny of the Majority: Fundamental Fairness in Representative Democracy* (New York: Free Press, 1994), 41–156.

6. Martin Luther King Jr., *A Testament of Hope: The Essential Writings of Martin Luther King, Jr.*, ed. James M. Washington (San Francisco: HarperCollins, 1986), 219.

7. Samuel P. Huntington, *American Politics: The Promise of Disharmony* (Cambridge: Belknap Press of Harvard University Press, 1981), 198.

8. *Shaw v. Reno*, 508 U.S. 630.

9. Several of these states elected African-American representatives during Reconstruction.

10. Hannah F. Pitkin, *The Concept of Representation* (Berkeley: University of California Press, 1967); Carol M. Swain, *Black Faces, Black Interests: The Representation of African Americans in Congress* (Cambridge: Harvard University Press, 1993), 5.

11. Earl Black and Merle Black, *Politics and Society in the South* (Cambridge: Harvard University Press, 1987), 143.

CHAPTER 2

1. William L. Clay, *Just Permanent Interests: Black Americans in Congress 1870–1992* (New York: Amistad Press, 1993), 12–44, 355–356, 359–402; Colleen McGuiness, ed., *American Leaders 1789–1991* (Washington, D.C.: Congressional Quarterly, 1991), 82–83; Norman J. Ornstein, Thomas E. Mann, and Michael J. Malbin, *Vital Statistics on Congress 1989–1990* (Washington, D.C.: Congressional Quarterly, 1990), 35; Swain, 21–28.

2. Black and Black, 3–5; John Dittmer, *Local People: The Struggle for Civil Rights in Mississippi* (Chicago: University of Illinois Press, 1994); V.O. Key, *Southern Politics in State and Nation* (Knoxville: University of Tennessee Press, 1949), 533–643; J. Morgan Kousser, *The Shaping of Southern Politics: Suffrage Restriction and the Establishment of the One-Party South 1880–1910* (New Haven: Yale University Press); Steven F. Lawson, *Black Ballots: Voting Rights in the South, 1944–1969* (New York: Columbia University Press, 1976), 4–22; Kay Mills, *This Little Light of Mine: The Life of Fannie Lou Hamer* (New York: Penguin, 1993).

3. McGuiness, 82. Republican Oscar DePriest represented Chicago in the House until his defeat by Democrat Arthur Mitchell in 1935. Democrat William L. Dawson

won the seat in 1943 and held it until 1970. Democrat Adam Clayton Powell represented the Harlem section of Manhattan in New York City from 1945 to 1971. Democrat Charles C. Diggs represented Detroit in the House from 1955 to 1980.

4. Nancy J. Weiss, *Farewell to the Party of Lincoln: Black Politics in the Age of FDR* (Princeton: Princeton University Press, 1983), 84–88.

5. McGuiness, 82–83. African-American Republican Edward W. Brooke represented Massachusetts in the Senate from 1967 to 1979.

6. *1890 United States Census*, Table 15, 402–434; Kenneth C. Martis, *The Historical Atlas of United States Congressional Districts 1789–1983* (New York: Free Press, 1982), 242, 257, 267, 275; Kenneth C. Martis, *The Historical Atlas of Political Parties in the United States Congress 1789–1989* (New York: Macmillan, 1989), 119–153; Terry Seip, *The South Returns to Congress* (Baton Rouge: Louisiana State University Press, 1983), 103–104; Swain, 21–22.

7. J. Morgan Kousser, "The Voting Rights Act and the Two Reconstructions," in *Controversies in Minority Voting Behavior: The Voting Rights Act in Perspective*, ed. Bernard Grofman and Chandler Davidson (Washington, D.C.: Brookings Institution, 1992), 144–151.

8. Kousser, "The Voting Rights Act and the Two Reconstructions," 154.

9. McGuiness, 85. New Mexico Democrat Joseph Montoya, who served from 1964 to 1977, remains the only other Latino elected to the Senate.

10. McGuiness, 82–83. All calculations exclude the non-voting delegates from the District of Columbia, American Samoa, Guam, and the Virgin Islands, and the resident commissioner from Puerto Rico.

11. McGuiness, 85.

12. Phil Duncan, ed., *Politics in America 1994: The 103rd Congress* (Washington, D.C.: Congressional Quarterly, 1993), 371–373, 379–380, 462–463, 994–995, 1055–1056, 1065–1067. Philip D. Duncan and Christine C. Lawrence, eds., *Politics in America 1996: The 104th Congress* (Washington, D.C.: Congressional Quarterly, 1995), 319–321, 327–328, 404–405, 856–857, 912–913, 922–923.

13. Census data on the Latino population of congressional districts prior to 1972 is unavailable.

14. The Ninth District of California, represented by Ron Dellums, is the exception. Asians slightly outnumber Latinos in this district.

15. Timothy G. O'Rourke, "The 1982 Amendments and the Voting Rights Paradox," in *Controversies in Minority Voting Behavior: The Voting Rights Act in Perspective*, ed. Bernard Grofman and Chandler Davidson (Washington, D.C.: Brookings Institution, 1992), 109; Swain, 198–204; Abigail Thernstrom, *Whose Votes Count? Affirmative Action and Minority Voting Rights* (Cambridge: Harvard University Press, 1987), 215–220.

16. Clark Bensen, *Polidata Election Reports: Congressional Districts, 103rd Congress*, vol. 1, *District-Level Returns for Congress and President for the 1992 General Election* (Lake Ridge, Va.: Polidata, 1993).

17. See chapter 1 for greater discussion of specific provisions of the Voting Rights Act, including Section 5.

18. Phil Duncan, ed., *Politics in America 1992: The 102nd Congress* (Congressional Quarterly, 1991), 8.

19. Steven F. Lawson, *In Pursuit of Power: Southern Blacks and Electoral Politics, 1965–1982* (New York: Columbia University Press, 1985), 203–208; Frank Parker, *Black Votes Count: Political Empowerment in Mississippi after 1965* (Chapel Hill: University of North Carolina Press, 1990), 41–51.

20. Grofman, Handley, and Niemi, 20.

21. Beth Donovan, "Key Man in Voting Rights Debate," *Congressional Quarterly Weekly Report*, 21 December 1991, 3691; Phil Duncan, "'Majority Minority' Mandate Will Reshape the House," *Congressional Quarterly Weekly Report*, 21 December 1991, 3689.

22. Swain, 170–189.

23. Rodolfo O. de la Garza et al., *Latino Voices: Mexican, Puerto Rican and Cuban Perspectives on American Politics* (San Francisco: Westview Press, 1992), 125.

24. David A. Bositis, *Redistricting and Representation: The Creation of Majority-Minority Districts and the Evolving Party System in the South* (Washington, D.C.: Joint Center for Political and Economic Studies, 1995), 26–35.

CHAPTER 3

1. O'Rourke, 109; Swain, 198–204; Thernstrom, 215–220.

2. Bernard Grofman and Lisa Handley, "Minority Population and Black and Hispanic Congressional Success in the 1970s and 1980s," *American Politics Quarterly* 17 (October 1989): 439–440. See also their discussion of black success in congressional elections in Lisa Handley and Bernard Grofman, "The Impact of the Voting Rights Act on Minority Representation: Black Officeholding in Southern State Legislatures and Congressional Delegations," in *Quiet Revolution in the South: The Impact of the Voting Rights Act 1965–1990* ed. Chandler Davidson and Bernard Grofman (Princeton: Princeton University Press, 1994), 343–344, 350.

3. Grofman and Handley, 441.

4. See, for example, Luis R. Fraga, "Latino Political Incorporation and the Voting Rights Act," in *Controversies in Minority Voting Behavior: The Voting Rights Act in Perspective*, ed. Bernard Grofman and Chandler Davidson (Washington, D.C.: Brookings Institution, 1992), 278–282; Kousser, "The Voting Rights Act and the Two Reconstructions," 173–176; Lawson, *In Pursuit of Power*, 161–163; Laughlin McDonald, "The 1982 Amendments of Section 2 and Minority Representation," in *Controversies in Minority Voting Behavior: The Voting Rights Act in Perspective*, ed. Bernard Grofman and Chandler Davidson (Washington, D.C.: Brookings Institution, 1992), 66–84; Parker, 194–196.

5. Thernstrom, 3, 23, 74–75, 154, 167–168, 215–216, 219–220, 226–227.

6. Swain, 207–217.

7. Data on race of representatives from *American Leaders, 1789–1991* (Washington, D.C.: Congressional Quarterly, 1991); *Politics in America*, various editions (Washington, D.C.: Congressional Quarterly). Data on percent black and Latino from the following Bureau of the Census publications: *Congressional District Data Book—93d Congress, 94th Congress*, Items 18, 40; *1980 Census of Population and Housing: Congressional Districts of the 98th Congress and Supplements*, Table 1; *1990 Census of Population and Housing: Population and Housing Characteristics for*

Congressional Districts of the 103rd Congress, Table 1; *1990 Census of Population and Housing: 104th Congress: Congressional Districts of the United States, Summary Tape Files 1D, 4D* (CD-ROM).

8. Barbara Jordan, Mickey Leland, Craig Washington, Yvonne Braithwaite Burke, Julian Dixon, Mervyn Dymally, Walter Tucker, Augustus Hawkins, Maxine Waters, Edolphus Towns, and Charles Rangel all won elections in districts with a majority-minority population, but without a black majority.

9. Redistricting prior to the 1992 election gave Dellums a majority-minority district for the first time. Together, African Americans, Latinos, and Asians compose a majority of the population in Dellums's district, so his last two victories were not in a white majority district.

10. Swain, 129–131.

11. Franks placed fifth and last on the first ballot at the 1990 Republican convention. Franks's share of the vote has never approached that of his white predecessor and ideological soulmate, Governor John Rowland. Rowland won the district with 54 percent of the vote in 1984, 61 percent in 1986 and 74 percent in 1988. George Bush received a higher share of the vote in the Fifth than in any other Connecticut district in both 1988 and 1992.

12. The majority of the voting-age population of Foglietta's district is not black.

13. Grofman and Handley, 439–440.

14. All but two of the coefficients shifted more than two standard errors between the two logits. Two of the coefficients with large negative coefficients and robust t-statistics in the first logit actually changed to positive coefficients in the second logit.

15. Grofman and Handley, 436–437, 444; Grofman, Handley, and Niemi, 120; Parker, 138–142, 203–204. For judicial decisions involving the 65 percent rule, see *Ketchum v. Byrne,* 740 F.2d 1528 (1984); *Kirksey v. Board of Supervisors of Hinds County,* 554 F.2d 139 (1977), and *United Jewish Organizations v. Carey,* 430 U.S. 144 (1977).

16. Grofman and Handley, 439–440; Parker, 138–142, 203–204; Swain, 195–197.

17. Parker, 51.

18. Raymond E. Wolfinger and Steven J. Rosenstone, *Who Votes?* (New Haven: Yale University Press, 1980), 17–20.

19. Duncan, ed., *Politics in America 1994: The 103rd Congress,* 1533–1534.

20. Duncan, ed., *Politics in America 1994: The 103rd Congress,* 1494.

21. Badillo and Garcia won election from the same district in New York City. After the 1990 redistricting, Torres' district became 62 percent Latino.

22. Only 11 percent of the voting-age population voted in the 1994 midterm congressional election.

23. See above discussion of the Second District of Mississippi for an exception to this statement.

24. Compare the bottom row of table 3.4 with the top row of table 3.2.

25. Among districts at least 40 percent Latino, 85 percent of residents have lived in the state for at least five years. Since the deviation from the total for all districts is quite small, the generalizations about all districts can be applied to the subset of Latino districts.

26. Swain, 184.

27. Duncan, ed., *Politics in America 1994: The 103rd Congress*, 462–463. It did not hurt Gutierrez one bit that he had endorsed Richard Daley in his successful quest for mayoralty. Daley not only pressured whites to leave the race, he encouraged whites to support Gutierrez in the Democratic primary over another Latino councilman, Juan Soliz, who had failed to support Daley's mayoral bid.

CHAPTER 4

1. Including unopposed candidates makes sense because the ability to scare off any major-party challenger implies a higher level of electoral security. Even though it skews the statistics in one direction, the statistics are at least skewed in the correct direction. Excluding unopposed candidates would mistakenly ignore the electoral security of unopposed incumbents and would result in vastly underestimating the security of groups with large number of unopposed incumbents.

2. Black and Black, 236–246, 261, 279.

3. Katherine Tate, *From Protest to Politics: The New Black Voters in American Elections* (Cambridge: Harvard University Press and Russell Sage Foundation, 1993), 52.

4. Tate, 52–53.

5. Edward G. Carmines and James A. Stimson, *Issue Evolution: Race and the Transformation of American Politics* (Princeton: Princeton University Press, 1989), 44–47.

6. de la Garza et al., 127.

7. de la Garza et al., 126.

8. de la Garza et al., 126.

9. Steven S. Smith, *Call to Order: Floor Politics in the House and Senate* (Washington, D.C.: Brookings Institution, 1989).

10. Lawson, *Black Ballots*, 158, 170, 196, 318–319.

11. Smith, 24–28.

12. McGuiness, 82–83. William Dawson, who had served since 1943, died in 1970, and Adam Clayton Powell retired in 1971 after being stripped of his committee chairmanship. Louis Stokes, William Clay, and Shirley Chisholm were elected in 1968. George Collins, Ron Dellums, Ralph Metcalfe, Parren Mitchell, and Charles Rangel won election in 1970.

13. Duncan and Lawrence, 254.

14. There is some anecdotal evidence that Democratic primaries are becoming more competitive in black majority districts. Bobby Rush handily defeated incumbent Charles Hayes in the First District of Illinois in 1992 after Hayes was declared one of the worst abusers in the House bank scandal. Mel Reynolds defeated incumbent Gus Savage on his third attempt in 1992 in an altered district that included more suburban white voters. In 1994, Sheila Jackson Lee defeated incumbent Craig Washington in the Eighteenth District of Texas with a biracial coalition of middle-class blacks and whites. Chaka Fattah unseated incumbent Lucien Blackwell in Pennsylvania's Second District. Barbara-Rose Collins failed to win renomination in the 1996 Democratic primary in Michigan's Fifteenth District.

15. Keith T. Poole and Howard Rosenthal, "Patterns of Congressional Voting," *American Journal of Political Science* 35 (February 1991): 235, 241–243.

16. Poole and Rosenthal, 230.

17. Northern Democrats and southern Democrats opposed each other on slavery in the nineteenth century and civil rights in the twentieth. Poole and Rosenthal discovered that the prediction of roll-call voting behavior on civil rights issues was significantly improved by the addition of the second dimension to the model between 1941 and 1971. The first, or party loyalty, dimension to their model was often orthogonal, and therefore irrelevant, to civil rights issues. Beginning in 1973, the first dimension increasingly did a better job of predicting the votes of individual legislators on civil rights issues. Agriculture replaced civil rights as the major second dimension issue. Although race internally divided the parties in earlier eras, the first Poole-Rosenthal score predicted votes on racial issues very well throughout the period studied here (1973–1992).

CHAPTER 5

1. Thernstrom. 23, 154.

2. Parker, 2.

3. Gerald David Jaynes and Robin M. Williams, Jr., eds., *A Common Destiny: Blacks and American Society* (Washington, D.C.: National Academy Press, 1989), 213; from the 1984 General Social Survey reported in Ann Kendrick, "The Core Economic Beliefs of Blacks and Whites" (paper prepared for the Committee on the Status of Black Americans, National Research Council, Washington, D.C., 1984).

4. Andrew Hacker, *Two Nations: Black and White, Separate, Hostile, Unequal* (New York: Ballantine, 1992), 94.

5. Howard Schuman, Charlotte Steeh, and Lawrence Bobo, *Racial Attitudes in America* (Cambridge: Harvard University Press, 1985), 141–142.

6. Tate, 57; from the 1984 National Black Election Study.

7. Tate, 52; from National Election Studies. Strong, weak, and independent party identifiers have been collapsed here.

8. "Portrait of the Electorate," *New York Times*, 5 November 1992, D9; from CBS/New York Times surveys. Floris W. Wood, ed., *An American Profile—Opinions and Behavior, 1972–1989* (New York: Gale Research, 1990), 1007, 1009.

9. Thomas Byrne Edsall and Mary D. Edsall, *Chain Reaction: The Impact of Race, Rights, and Taxes on American Politics* (New York: W.W. Norton, 1992), 160–161.

10. Gary King, *Unifying Political Methodology* (New York: Cambridge University Press, 1989), 8–10.

11. Poole and Rosenthal scaled the scores for the 100th–104th Congresses differently than for previous Congresses. After consulting with Keith Poole, I used regression analysis to find parameters to map the scores for the 100th–104th Congresses on to previous Congresses.

12. The distribution of the residuals across different levels of proportion black served as a test of how well the model uses race to fit ideology. Around two-thirds of the residuals should lie within 1σ of the predicted values and around 95 percent should lie within 2σ of the predicted values. The model meets this test well; 71 percent of the residuals lie within 1σ of the prediction line and 95 percent lie within 2σ of the prediction line. The residuals were broken into groups at intervals of 10 percent black in order to subject the model to greater scrutiny. Except for the group be-

tween 40 and 50 percent black, the residuals for all groups follow the general pattern of the whole. Though it differs from the overall pattern somewhat, the group between 40 percent and 50 percent does not seem to require rejection of the model. Only 53 percent of the group's residuals lie within 1σ of the prediction line, but 96 percent lie within 2σ of the same line. An alternative model with a slope and intercept shift at 50 percent black fails the residuals test because almost all of the residuals fall below the prediction line between 40 percent and 50 percent black. This result suggests that the model with a slope and intercept shift at 40 percent black more accurately reflects the relationship between race and ideology.

13. De la Garza et al., 84–90.

14. Anthony Downs, *An Economic Theory of Democracy* (New York: Harper and Row, 1957); Robert Erikson, "The Electoral Impact of Congressional Roll Call Voting," *American Political Science Review* 65 (1971): 1018–1032; Morris P. Fiorina, *Representatives, Roll Calls, and Constituencies* (Lexington: D.C. Heath, 1974), 33–34; Samuel Huntington, "A Revised Theory of American Party Politics," *American Political Science Review* 2 (1980): 91–106.

15. This specification is substantially more complex than other recent models of the effect of racial composition of a district's population on ideology. In her linear regression models of interest-group ratings, Carol Swain includes only four independent variables: party, region, percent urban, and percent black. See Swain, 16. In their study of mean ADA scores, Grofman, Griffin, and Glazer control only for region and party. See Bernard Grofman, Robert Griffin, and Amihai Glazer, "The Effect of Black Population on Electing Democrats and Liberals to the House of Representatives," *Legislative Studies Quarterly* 17 (August 1992) 365–379. In his analysis of the impact of redistricting on the roll-call voting behavior of southern representatives, Charles Bullock controls for many political characteristics of representatives, but percent black is the only constituency variable included in his linear regression models. See Charles S. Bullock, III, "The Impact of Changing the Racial Composition of Congressional Districts on Legislators' Roll Call Behavior" (paper presented at the Hendricks Symposium, University of Nebraska, Lincoln, April 8–9, 1994).

16. The pooled model for all Congresses does a good job of modeling the entire time period. Disaggregating the data by Congress indicates that representatives from districts less than 40 percent black consistently respond to the presence of African Americans at around the same rate across all Congresses. The coefficient on percent black for the analysis of each separate Congress remains within two standard errors of the coefficients for the separate analyses of of the other Congresses as well as for the model of all Congresses. The coefficients on 40 percent black district and percent black for districts greater than 40 percent black in the pooled model similarly lie within two standard errors of the corresponding coefficients for the analyses of individual Congresses.

17. See below in this chapter in this chpater for more information on the relative impact of changing the party of a district's representative compared to altering its racial composition.

18. Charles Bullock III, "Congressional Voting and the Mobilization of a Black Electorate in the South," *Journal of Politics* 43 (1981): 662–682; Mary Herring, "Legislative Responsiveness to Black Constituents in Three Deep South States," *Journal of Politics* 52 (1990): 740–758; Robert Huckfeldt and Carol Weitzel Kohfeld, *Race*

and the Decline of Class in American Politics (Chicago: University of Illinois Press, 1989), 50; Key, 42–244, 319–325; Kenny J. Whitby and Franklin D. Gilliam Jr., "A Longitudinal Analysis of Competing Explanations for the Transformation of Southern Congressional Politics," *Journal of Politics* 53 (1991): 504–518.

19. Parabolic and cubic curves provide one way to model the relationship between the racial composition of a district and ideology if white backlash prevents African Americans from gaining stronger influence with greater numbers in white majority districts. The parabolic model contains two racial terms to model its one bend: *proportion black* and *(proportion black)²*. The positive slope of the curve in white majority districts in the parabolic model reflects that increasing white conservatism forces representatives to cast more conservative roll-call votes as the black population rises in order to avoid losing reelection at the hands of an increasingly conservative white electorate. The curve turns downward around 50 percent black because whites cannot prevent the election of liberal representatives in black majority districts.

The cubic model requires three terms to model a slightly more complex white reaction using its two bends: *proportion black*, *(proportion black)²*, and *(proportion black)³*. This model assumes little white backlash in areas with few blacks as the black population rises, so representatives feel free to cast more liberal votes on the House floor as the population rises in these districts. Once the black population attains a certain size, however, whites feel threatened and start voting more conservatively with further black population increases. The slope of the curve turns positive because white conservatism forces representatives to act more conservatively in order to maintain their electoral coalition. As with the parabolic model, the curve turns downward again when blacks achieve majority status and gain control of the district.

Statistical analysis reveals that neither the parabolic nor the cubic white backlash models fit the data. White backlash is not strong enough to impede representatives from casting more liberal roll-call votes as the percentage of blacks rises. Neither of the curves has the positive slope predicted by white backlash models for at least some of the white majority districts. The negative slope indicates that members of Congress respond to the presence of African Americans even in white majority districts.

The parabolic and cubic models provided useful clues for constructing a more accurate model despite not fitting the data well. The consistently negative slope of the curves and the absence of sizable bends in both models suggested that a linear model might better reflect the actual relationship between race and ideology. Disproportionate numbers of the residuals fell below the prediction lines for districts between 40 and 50 percent black in plots of both models. Introducing slope and intercept shifts into the simple linear model at 40 percent black models this disjuncture. In short, the problems with the parabolic and cubic white backlash models lead toward the adoption of a linear with with slope and intercept shifts at 40 percent black.

20. Carmines and Stimson.

21. David Epstein and Sharon O'Halloran, "Do Majority-Minority Districts Maximize Substantive Black Representation in Congress?" (manuscript, Columbia University, 1996).

22. Swain 1993, 16–19, 211–215.

23. Table 5.3 displays the predicted shift in conservatism at 40 percent black and the predicted effect of a 10 percent increase in the black population above and below the 40 percent black threshold. The effect of altering the racial composition of a district can be calculated relatively easily from these predicted values. Raising the black population from 35 percent to 65 percent equals: .5(10 percent increase below 40 percent black) + (shift at 40 percent black) + 2.5(10 percent increase above 40 percent black). Plugging in the predicted values for northern Democrats reveals that increasing the black share of the population from 35 percent to 65 percent equals: .5(−.0084) + (−.1395) + 2.5(−.0073) = −.16. Similarly, plugging in the predicted values for southern Democrats equals: .5(−.0292) + (−.1425) + 2.5(−.0302) = −.23.

24. The impact of changing the party of the representative was calculated by comparing the total effect of the coefficients involving Democrats with the total effect of coefficients involving Republicans for the model presented in table 5.1. The total effect of the coefficients involving Republicans equals: .53(proportion high school graduates) + .003(first year elected). The total effect of the coefficients involving Democrats equals: .13 − .73(proportion Latino) + .07(south) + .03(margin of victory). In calculating the total impact of the coefficients in each region, the various demographic variables were held constant at the mean for representatives elected in that region in 1992. Plugging in reveals the total impact of being a northern Republican equals: .53(.77) + .0034(83.37) = .69. The total impact of being a northern Democrat equals: .13 − .73(.09) + .07(0) + .03(.31) = .07. Subtracting the effect of being a northern Democrat from being a northern Republican reveals that switching from a Democrat to a Republican in the North makes representatives .62 points more conservative on the Poole-Rosenthal scale. The total impact of being a southern Republican equals: .53(.71) + .0034(83.86) = .66. The total impact of being a southern Democrat equals: .13 − .73(.09) + .07(1) + .03(.32) = .14. Changing from a Democrat to a Republican results in the election of a representative .52 points more conservative on the Poole-Rosenthal scale.

25. Grofman, 1237–1276; Swain 1995, 227.

26. Grofman and Handley, 436–445.

27. Grofman, Griffin, and Glazer, 365–379.

28. Unlike other Latinos, Cuban Americans provide strong support for Republican candidates (see de la Garza et al.). The poll results for all Latinos undoubtedly understimate support for the Democrats among northern Latinos since most Cuban Americans live in south Florida.

29. Examining changes in the link between race and ideology over time only reinforces these conclusions. Responsiveness to blacks actually increases in years, such as 1980, in which the Republicans have their greatest electoral successes. White southern Democrats must show greater sensitivity to white opinion in relatively conservative years or risk being turned out of office on the Republican tide. Even in good years for the Democrats, such as 1982, white southern Democrats pay close attention to the share of the electorate composed by blacks and whites. Savvy southern white Democratic politicians must demonstrate acute awareness of the vicissitudes of white opinion in order to regularly win reelection in a constantly changing political climate.

CHAPTER 6

1. Swain, *Black Faces, Black Interests*, 218.

2. Bernard Grofman, "Would Vince Lombardi Have Been Right If He Had Said: 'When It Comes to Redistricting, Race Isn't Everything, It's the *Only* Thing'?" *Cardozo Law Review* 14 (1993): 1249–1256.

3. Grofman, "Would Vince Lombardi Have Been Right," 1253–1254.

4. Bernard Grofman, "*Shaw v. Reno* and the Future of Voting Rights," *PS: Political Science and Politics* 28 (March 1995): 27.

5. Grofman, "*Shaw v. Reno*," 27.

6. Parker, 43–52, 140; Swain, 80–81.

7. Michael Barone and Grant Ujifusa, *The Almanac of American Politics 1994* (Washington, D.C.: National Journal, 1994), 7.

8. Swain, *Black Faces, Black Interests*, 22.

9. Duncan, *Politics in America 1994*, 1120–1121.

10. Barone and Ujifusa, *The Almanac of American Politics 1994*, 942, 968–969.

11. Representative Connie Morella of Maryland's Eighth District probably constitutes the only exception.

12. Kevin Hill, "Does the Creation of Majority Black Districts Aid Republicans? An Analysis of the 1992 Congressional Elections in Eight Southern States," *Journal of Politics* 57 (May 1995): 384–401.

13. NAACP Legal Defense and Educational Fund, "The Effect of Section 2 of the Voting Rights Act on the 1994 Congressional Elections," 30 November 1994.

14. In his examination of the impact of racial redistricting on the outcome of the 1992 elections in the South, Hill (1995) limited his analysis to seats won by the Democrats in 1990 so Alabama's Second District was beyond the purview of his study.

15. Swain, *Black Faces, Black Interests*, 228–234; Carol M. Swain, "The Future of Black Representation," *American Prospect* (Fall 1995): 78–83; confirmed by David Bositis, telephone conversation, 15 September 1995.

16. Charles S. Bullock III, "Affirmative Action Districts: In Whose Faces Will They Blow Up?" *Campaigns and Elections* (April 1995): 22–23; Michael Kelly, "Segregation Anxiety," *New Yorker*, 20 November 1995, 43–54. Bullock also notes (p. 22): "All districts held by Democrats in 1991 in which redistricting reduced the black percentage by more than 10 points have now fallen to Republicans. The GOP took four of these districts in 1992 and two more in 1994."

17. Lisa Handley, Bernard Grofman and Wayne Arden, "Electing Minority Preferred Candidates to Legislative Office: The Relationship between Minority Percentages in Districts and the Election of Minority Preferred Candidates," *National Political Science Review* (1996); cited in Bernard Grofman, Lisa Handley, and Robert Griffin, "Is the Voting Rights Act a Villain? Linking Empirical Beliefs and Normative Judgements" (paper presented at the Annual Meeting of the American Political Science Association, Chicago, 31 August–3 September 1995).

18. John R. Petrocik and Scott W. Desposato, "The Partisan Consequence of Majority-Minority Redistricting in the South, 1992 and 1994" (paper presented at the Annual Meeting of the American Political Science Association, Chicago, 31 August–3 September 1995). The abstract to the paper states: "MM districting wouldn't have defeated many Democratic incumbents if the election tide had been

less hostile to the Democrats." One could reasonably conclude from this statement that more Democrats would have survived the Republican tide if racial redistricting had not occurred. Even if racial redistricting mattered because of the magnitude of the Republican tide, the important point is that the Democrats would have won more seats despite the Republican tide if racial redistricting had not concentrated black voters.

19. Richard L. Engstrom, "Voting Rights Districts: Debunking the Myths," *Campaigns and Elections* (April 1995): 24, 46.

20. Swain, *Black Faces, Black Interests*, 231–232, and Bositis, telephone conversation, 15 September 1995, are both highly critical of the LDF Report.

21. Gary C. Jacobson, "The 1994 House Elections in Perspective" (paper presented at the Annual Meeting of the Midwest Political Science Association, Chicago, 6–8 April 1995).

22. Only Engstrom contends that racial redistricting does not account for the loss of any seats in North Carolina in 1994. The LDF Report concedes that the Democrats probably would have won the Third District of North Carolina if racial redistricting had not reduced the number of black voters in the district.

CHAPTER 7

1. *Shaw v. Reno*, No. 92–357, 509 U.S. 630, 125 L. Ed. 2s 511 (1993).

2. *Johnson v. Miller*, 1994 U.S. Dist. Lexis 13043. See the dissent in *Johnson v. Miller* as well as Pildes and Niemi for comparisons between Georgia's Eleventh District and other congressional districts.

3. *Miller v. Johnson*, 1995 U.S. Lexis 4462; Joan Biskupic, "Court Rejects Race-Based Voting District: Georgia Plan Invalidated in 5–4 Ruling," *Washington Post*, 30 June 1995, A1, A18; Kenneth J. Cooper, "Minorities in Congress Fear Loss of Diversity: Others Question Ruling's Effect Beyond Georgia," *Washington Post*, 30 June 1995, A18; Linda Greenhouse, "Justices, In 5–4 Vote, Reject Districts Drawn with Race the 'Predominant Factor,'" *New York Times*, 30 June 1995, A1, A13; Steven A. Holmes, "Voting Rights Experts Say Challenges to Political Maps Cause Turmoil," *New York Times*, 30 June 1995, A13; Holly Idelson, "Court Takes a Harder Line On Minority Voting Blocs," *Congressional Quarterly Weekly Report*, 1 July 1995, 1944–1946.

4. Biskupic, A18.

5. *Miller v. Johnson*, 1995 U.S. Lexis 4462, 26.

6. *Miller v. Johnson*, 1995 U.S. Lexis 4462, 22.

7. *Miller v. Johnson*, 1995 U.S. Lexis 4462, 11.

8. *Miller v. Johnson*, 1995 U.S. Lexis 4462, 21–23. See also Justice Stevens's dissenting opinion in *U.S. v. Hays*, 1995 U.S. Lexis 4464, 7–8, Justice White's dissenting opinion in *Shaw v. Reno*, and William Raspberry, "No More Blacks in Congress?" *Washington Post*, 30 June 1995, A23.

9. *Miller v. Johnson*, 1995 U.S. Lexis 4462, 20; see also Allan Lichtman's comment in Cooper, A18.

10. *DeWitt v. Wilson* (856 F. Supp. 1409); Idelson, 1945.

11. *Shaw v. Hunt*, 1994 U.S. Dist. Lexis 11102, 154.

12. *Vera v. Richards*, 1994 U.S. Dist. Lexis 12334, 30.

13. Grofman, Handley, and Niemi, 49; *Thornburg v. Gingles*, 478 U.S. 30, 50–51.

14. *Miller v. Johnson*, 1995 U.S. Lexis 4462, 21.

15. Juliana Gruenwald, "Panel Redraws Texas Map, Sets Election Date," *Congressional Quarterly Weekly Report*, 10 August 1996, 2270.

16. *Hays v. Louisiana (Hays I)*, No. 92-CV-1522; Dave Kaplan, "Louisiana Ruling May Offer Guidelines for Other Cases," *Congressional Quarterly Weekly Report*, 8 January 1994, 29–31.

17. *Hays v. Louisiana (Hays II)*; Dave Kaplan, "Majority Black District Rejected in Louisiana," *Congressional Quarterly Weekly Report*, 30 July 1994, 2175; Dave Kaplan, "Redrawn Map Still Features Two Minority Districts," *Congressional Quarterly Weekly Report*, 30 April 1994, 1083–1084.

18. *U.S. v. Hays*, 1995 U.S. Lexis 4464.

19. Juliana Gruenwald, 1948; *Hays v. Louisiana* (1996), U.S. District Court, Western District of Louisiana, Shreveport Division, No. 92–1522, No. 95–1241.

20. Holmes, A13; Ronald Smothers, "G.O.P. Anxiously Awaits Redistricting," *New York Times*, 30 June 1995, A13.

21. Gruenwald, "Court Ruling Expected to Spark More Suits," 1948.

REFERENCES

BOOKS

Barone, Michael, and Grant Ujifusa. *The Almanac of American Politics*, various editions. Washington, D.C.: National Journal.

Bensen, Clark. *Polidata Election Reports: Congressional Districts, 103rd Congress.* Vol. 1, *District-Level Returns for Congress and President for the 1992 General Election*. Lake Ridge, Va.: Polidata, 1993.

Black, Earl, and Merle Black. *Politics and Society in the South*. Cambridge: Harvard University Press, 1987.

Bositis, David A. *Redistricting and Representation: The Creation of Majority-Minority Districts and the Evolving Party System in the South*. Washington, D.C.: Joint Center for Political and Economic Studies, 1995.

Carmines, Edward G., and James A. Stimson. *Issue Evolution: Race and the Transformation of American Politics*. Princeton: Princeton University Press, 1989.

Clausen, Aage. *How Congressmen Decide*. New York: St. Martin's Press, 1973.

Clay, William L. *Just Permanent Interests: Black Americans in Congress 1870–1992*. New York: Amistad Press, 1993.

Davidson, Chandler, and Bernard Grofman, eds. *Quiet Revolution in the South: The Impact of the Voting Rights Act 1965–1990*. Princeton: Princeton University Press, 1994.

de la Garza, Rodolfo O., Louis DeSipio, F. Chris Garcia, John Garcia, and Angelo Falcon. *Latino Voices: Mexican, Puerto Rican and Cuban Perspectives on American Politics*. San Francisco: Westview Press, 1992.

Dittmer, John. *Local People: The Struggle for Civil Rights in Mississippi*. Chicago: University of Illinois Press, 1994.

Downs, Anthony. *An Economic Theory of Democracy*. New York: Harper and Row, 1957.

Duncan, Phil, ed. *Politics in America*, various editions. Washington, D.C.: Congressional Quarterly.

Duncan, Philip D., and Christine C. Lawrence, eds. *Politics in America 1996: The 104th Congress*. Washington, D.C.: Congressional Quarterly, 1995.

Edsall, Thomas Byrne, and Mary D. Edsall. *Chain Reaction: The Impact of Race, Rights, and Taxes on American Politics*. New York: W.W. Norton, 1992.

Erie, Steven P. *Rainbow's End: Irish-Americans and the Dilemmas of Urban Machine Politics, 1840–1985*. Berkeley: University of California Press, 1988.

Fiorina, Morris P. *Representatives, Roll Calls, and Constituencies*. Lexington, Mass.: D.C. Heath, 1974.

Fraga, Luis R. "Latino Political Incorporation and the Voting Rights Act." In *Controversies in Minority Voting Behavior: The Voting Rights Act in Perspective*, edited by Bernard Grofman and Chandler Davidson, 278–282. Washington, D.C.: Brookings Institution, 1992.

Grofman, Bernard, Lisa Handley, and Richard G. Niemi. *Minority Representation and the Quest for Voting Equality*. New York: Cambridge University Press, 1992.

Guinier, Lani. *The Tyranny of the Majority: Fundamental Fairness in Representative Democracy*. New York: Free Press, 1994.

Hacker, Andrew. *Two Nations: Black and White, Separate, Hostile, Unequal*. New York: Ballantine, 1992.

Handley, Lisa, and Bernard Grofman. "The Impact of the Voting Rights Act on Minority Representation: Black Officeholding in Southern State Legislatures and Congressional Delegations." In *Quiet Revolution in the South: The Impact of the Voting Rights Act 1965–1990*, edited by Chandler Davidson and Bernard Grofman, 351–377. Princeton: Princeton University Press, 1994.

Huckfeldt, Robert, and Carol Weitzel Kohfeld. *Race and the Decline of Class in American Politics*. Chicago: University of Illinois Press, 1989.

Huntington, Samuel P. *American Politics: The Promise of Disharmony*. Cambridge: Belknap Press of Harvard University Press, 1981.

Jaynes, Gerald David, and Robin M. Williams, eds. *A Common Destiny: Blacks and American Society*. Washington, D.C.: National Academy Press, 1989.

Kendrick, Ann. "The Core Economic Beliefs of Blacks and Whites." Paper prepared for the Committee on the Status of Black Americans, National Research Council, Washington, D.C., 1984.

Key, V. O. *Southern Politics in State and Nation*. Knoxville: University of Tennessee Press, 1949.

King, Gary. *Unifying Political Methodology*. New York: Cambridge University Press, 1989.

King Jr., Martin Luther. *A Testament of Hope: The Essential Writings of Martin Luther King, Jr.*, edited by James M. Washington. San Francisco: HarperCollins, 1986.

Kingdon, John W. *Congressmen's Voting Decisions*. Ann Arbor: University of Michigan Press, 1989.

Kousser, J. Morgan. *The Shaping of Southern Politics: Suffrage Restriction and the Establishment of the One-Party South 1880–1910*. New Haven: Yale University Press, 1974.

————. "The Voting Rights Act and the Two Reconstructions." In *Controversies in Minority Voting Behavior: The Voting Rights Act in Perspective*, edited by Bernard Grofman and Chandler Davidson, 135–176. Washington, D.C.: Brookings Institution, 1992.

Lawson, Steven F. *Black Ballots: Voting Rights in the South, 1944–1969*. New York: Columbia University Press, 1976.

————. *In Pursuit of Power: Southern Blacks and Electoral Politics, 1965–1982*. New York: Columbia University Press, 1985.

Martis, Kenneth C. *The Historical Atlas of United States Congressional Districts 1789–1983*. New York: Free Press, 1982.

————. *The Historical Atlas of Political Parties in the United States Congress 1789–1989*. New York: Macmillan, 1989.

Mayhew, David R. *Congress: the Electoral Connection*. New Haven: Yale University Press, 1974.

McDonald, Laughlin. "The 1982 Amendments of Section 2 and Minority Representation." In *Controversies in Minority Voting Behavior: The Voting Rights Act in*

Perspective, edited by Bernard Grofman and Chandler Davidson, 66–84. Washington, D.C.: Brookings Institution, 1992.

McGuiness, Colleen, ed. *American Leaders 1789–1991*. Washington, D.C.: Congressional Quarterly, 1991.

Mills, Kay. *This Little Light of Mine: The Life of Fannie Lou Hamer*. New York: Penguin, 1993.

Ornstein, Norman J., Thomas E. Mann, and Michael J. Malbin. *Vital Statistics on Congress 1989–1990*. Washington, D.C.: Congressional Quarterly, 1990.

O'Rourke, Timothy G. "The 1982 Amendments and the Voting Rights Paradox." In *Controversies in Minority Voting Behavior: The Voting Rights Act in Perspective*, edited by Bernard Grofman and Chandler Davidson, 85–113. Washington, D.C.: Brookings Institution, 1992.

Parker, Frank. *Black Votes Count: Political Empowerment in Mississippi after 1965*. Chapel Hill: University of North Carolina Press, 1990.

Pitkin, Hannah F. *The Concept of Representation*. Berkeley: University of California Press, 1967.

Schuman, Howard, Charlotte Steeh, and Lawrence Bobo. *Racial Attitudes in America*. Cambridge: Harvard University Press, 1985.

Seip, Terry. *The South Returns to Congress*. Baton Rouge: Louisiana State University Press, 1983.

Smith, Steven S. *Call to Order: Floor Politics in the House and Senate*. Washington, D.C.: Brookings Institution, 1989.

Swain, Carol M. *Black Faces, Black Interests: The Representation of African Americans in Congress*. Cambridge: Harvard University Press, 1993, updated 1995.

Tate, Katherine. *From Protest to Politics: The New Black Voters in American Elections*. Cambridge: Harvard University Press and Russell Sage Foundation, 1993.

Thernstrom, Abigail. *Whose Votes Count? Affirmative Action and Minority Voting Rights*. Cambridge: Harvard University Press, 1987.

Weiss, Nancy J. *Farewell to the Party of Lincoln: Black Politics in the Age of FDR*. Princeton: Princeton University Press, 1983.

Wolfinger, Raymond E., and Steven J. Rosenstone. *Who Votes?* New Haven: Yale University Press, 1980.

Wood, Floris W., ed. *An American Profile—Opinions and Behavior, 1972–1989*. New York: Gale Research, 1990.

SCHOLARLY JOURNALS AND PAPERS

Bullock III, Charles S. "Congressional Voting and the Mobilization of a Black Electorate in the South." *Journal of Politics* 43 (1981): 662–682.

————. "The Impact of Changing the Racial Composition of Congressional Districts on Legislators' Roll Call Behavior." Paper presented at the Hendricks Symposium, University of Nebraska, Lincoln, 8–9 April 1994.

Epstein, David, and Sharon O'Halloran. "Do Majority-Minority Districts Maximize Substantive Black Representation in Congress?" Manuscript, Columbia University, 1996.

Erikson, Robert. "The Electoral Impact of Congressional Roll Call Voting." *American Political Science Review* 65 (1971): 1018–1032.

Gopoian, J. David, and Darrell M. West. "Trading Security for Seats: Strategic Considerations in the Redistricting Process." *Journal of Politics* 46 (1984): 1080–1096.

Bernard Grofman. "Would Vince Lombardi Have Been Right If He Had Said: 'When It Comes to Redistricting, Race Isn't Everything, It's the *Only* Thing'?" *Cardozo Law Review* 14 (April 1993): 1237–1276.

———. "*Shaw v. Reno* and the Future of Voting Rights." *PS: Political Science and Politics* 28 (March 1995): 27–36.

Grofman, Bernard, Robert Griffin, and Amihai Glazer. "The Effect of Black Population on Electing Democrats and Liberals to the House of Representatives." *Legislative Studies Quarterly* 17 (August 1992): 365–379.

Grofman, Bernard, and Lisa Handley. "Minority Population and Black and Hispanic Congressional Success in the 1970s and 1980s." *American Politics Quarterly* 17 (October 1989): 436–445.

Grofman, Bernard, Lisa Handley, and Robert Griffin. "Is the Voting Rights Act a Villain? Linking Empirical Beliefs and Normative Judgements." Paper presented at the Annual Meeting of the American Political Science Association, Chicago, 31 August–3 September 1995.

Handley, Lisa, Bernard Grofman, and Wayne Arden. "Electing Minority Preferred Candidates to Legislative Office: The Relationship between Minority Percentages in Districts and the Election of Minority Preferred Candidates." *National Political Science Review* (1996).

Herring, Mary. "Legislative Responsiveness to Black Constituents in Three Deep South States." *Journal of Politics* 52 (1990): 740–758.

Hill, Kevin. "Does the Creation of Majority Black Districts Aid Republicans? An Analysis of the 1992 Congressional Elections in Eight Southern States." *Journal of Politics* 57 (May 1995): 384–401.

Huntington, Samuel. "A Revised Theory of American Party Politics." *American Political Science Review* 2 (1980): 91–106.

Jacobson, Gary C. "The 1994 House Elections in Perspective." Paper presented at the Annual Meeting of the Midwest Political Science Association, Chicago, 6–8 April 1995.

Karlan, Pamela S. "Après *Shaw* le déluge?" *PS: Political Science and Politics* 28 (March 1995): 50–54.

MacManus, Susan A. "The Appropriateness of Biracial Approaches to Measuring the Fairness of Representation in a Multicultural World." *PS: Political Science and Politics* 28 (March 1995): 42–47.

McClain, Paula D., and Joseph Stewart, Jr. "W(h)ither the Voting Rights Act After *Shaw v. Reno*: Advancing to the Past?" *PS: Political Science and Politics* 28 (March 1995): 24–26.

NAACP Legal Defense and Educational Fund, "The Effect of Section 2 of the Voting Rights Act on the 1994 Congressional Elections," 30 November 1994.

O'Rourke, Timothy G. "*Shaw v. Reno* and the *Hunt* for Double Cross-Overs" *PS: Political Science and Politics* 28 (March 1995): 36–41.

Parker, Frank R. "*Shaw v. Reno*: A Constitutional Setback for Minority Representation." *PS: Political Science and Politics* 28 (March 1995): 47–50.

Petrocik, John R., and Scott W. Desposato. "The Partisan Consequence of Majority-Minority Redistricting in the South, 1992 and 1994." Paper presented at the Annual Meeting of the American Political Science Association, Chicago, 31 August–3 September 1995.

Pildes, Richard H., and Richard G. Niemi. "Expressive Harms, 'Bizarre Districts,' and Voting Rights: Evaluating Election-District Appearances after *Shaw v. Reno*." *Michigan Law Review* 92 (December 1993): 483–587.

Pinderhughes, Dianne M. "The Voting Rights Act—Whither History?" *PS: Political Science and Politics* 28 (March 1995): 55–56.

Poole, Keith, and Howard Rosenthal. "Patterns of Congressional Voting." *American Journal of Political Science* 35 (February 1991): 228–278.

Polsby, Daniel D., and Robert D. Popper. "Ugly: An Inquiry Into the Problem of Racial Gerrymandering Under the Voting Rights Act." *Michigan Law Review* 92 (December 1993): 652–682.

Weisberg, Herbert. "Evaluating Theories of Congressional Roll-Call Voting." *American Political Science Review* 22 (1978): 560–570.

Whitby, Kenny J., and Franklin D. Gilliam Jr. "A Longitudinal Analysis of Competing Explanations for the Transformation of Southern Congressional Politics." *Journal of Politics* 53 (1991): 504–518.

NEWSPAPERS AND PERIODICALS

Applebome, Peter. "Suit Challenging Redrawn Districts That Help Blacks." *New York Times*, 14 February 1994, A1, A14.

———. "Guinier Ideas, Once Seen as Odd, Now Get Serious Study." *New York Times*, 3 April 1994, E5.

Benenson, Bob. "Republicans Score Big Win with Illinois Map." *Congressional Quarterly Weekly Report*, 9 November 1991, 3326.

———. "GOP's Dreams of a Comeback Via the New Map Dissolve." *Congressional Quarterly Weekly Report*, 7 November 1992, 3580–3581.

Biskupic, Joan. "Court Rejects Race-Based Voting District: Georgia Plan Invalidated in 5–4 Ruling." *Washington Post*, 30 June 1995, A1, A18.

Bullock III, Charles S. "Affirmative Action Districts: In Whose Faces Will They Blow Up?" *Campaigns and Elections* (April 1995): 22–23

Cooper, Kenneth J. "Minorities in Georgia Fear Loss of Diversity: Others Question Ruling's Effect Beyond Georgia." *Washington Post*, 30 June 1995, A18.

Donovan, Beth. "Nation Watches as Texas Struggles to Create Minority Districts." *Congressional Quarterly Weekly Report*, 17 August 1991, 2293–2295.

———. "Voting Rights Act, Lawsuits Result in Many Delays." *Congressional Quarterly Weekly Report*, 9 November 1991, 3323–3325.

———. "Key Man in Voting Rights Debate." *Congressional Quarterly Weekly Report*, 21 December 1991, 3691.

———. "Political Dance Played Out Through Legal Wrangling." *Congressional Quarterly Weekly Report*, 21 December 1991, 3690–3695.

Duncan, Phil. "'Majority Minority' Mandate Will Reshape the House." *Congressional Quarterly Weekly Report*, 21 December 1991, 3689.

Engstrom, Richard L. "Voting Rights Districts: Debunking the Myths." *Campaigns and Elections* (April 1995): 24, 46.

Greenhouse, Linda. "Justices in 5–4 Vote, Reject Districts Drawn with Race the 'Predominant Factor.'" *New York Times*, 30 June 1995, A1, A13.

Gruenwald, Juliana. "Court Ruling Expected to Spark More Suits." *Congressional Quarterly Weekly Report*, 1 July 1995, 1947–1948.

———. "Panel Redraws Texas Map, Sets Election Date." *Congressional Quarterly Weekly Report*, 10 August 1996, 2270.

Holmes, Steven A. "Voting Rights Experts Say Challenges to Political Maps Cause Turmoil." *New York Times*, 30 June 1995, A13.

Idelson, Holly. "Court Takes a Harder Line On Minority Voting Blocs." *Congressional Quarterly Weekly Report*, 1 July 1995, 1944–1946.

Kaplan, Dave. "Louisiana Ruling May Offer Guidelines for Other Cases." *Congressional Quarterly Weekly Report*, 8 January 1994, 29–31.

———. "Redrawn Map Still Features Two Minority Districts." *Congressional Quarterly Weekly Report*, 30 April 1994, 1083–1084.

———. "Majority Black District Rejected in Louisiana." *Congressional Quarterly Weekly Report* , July 30, 1994, 2175.

Kelly, Michael. "Segregation Anxiety." *New Yorker*, 20 November 1995, 43–54.

"Portrait of the Electorate." *New York Times*, 5 November 1992, D9.

Raspberry, William. "No More Blacks in Congress?" *Washington Post*, 30 June 1995, A23.

Smothers, Ronald. "G.O.P. Anxiously Awaits Redistricting." *New York Times*, 30 June 1995, A13.

Sunstein, Cass R. "Voting Rites." *New Republic*, 25 April 1994.

"Supreme Court Allows Use of Louisiana Map in 1994." *Congressional Quarterly Weekly Report*, 13 August 1994, 2373.

Swain, Carol M. "Black-Majority Districts: A Bad Idea." *New York Times*, 3 June 1993, A21.

———. "The Future of Black Representation." *American Prospect* (Fall 1995): 78–83

Thernstrom, Abigail. "Guinier Miss." *New Republic*, 14 June 1993, 16–19.

COURT CASES

Allen v. State Board of Elections, 393 U.S. 544 (1969).

Armour v. State of Ohio, 895 F.2d 1078 (6th Cir. 1990).

Baker v. Carr, 369 U.S. 186 (1962).

Beer v. United States, 425 U.S. 130 (1976).

Bush v. Vera, 1996 WL 315857 (1996).

City of Mobile v. Bolden, 446 U.S. 55 (1980).

De Witt v. Wilson, 856 F. Supp. 1409.

Garza v. Los Angeles County Board of Supervisors, 918 F.2d 763 (9th Cir. 1990).

Hays v. Louisiana (Hays I), 839 F. Supp. 1188 (1993).

Hays v. Louisiana (Hays II) 862 F. Supp. 119 (1994).

Hays v. Louisiana, U.S. District Court, Western District of Louisiana, Shreveport Division, No. 92–1522, No. 95–1241 (1996).

Johnson v. Miller, U.S. Dist. Lexis 13043 (1994).

Ketchum v. Byrne, 740 F.2d 1398 (7th Cir. 1984).

Kirksey v. Board of Supervisors of Hinds County, 554 F.2d 139 (1977).

Miller v. Johnson, 1995 U.S. Lexis 4462 (1995).

NAACP v. Schaefer, 849 F. Supp. 1022 (1995).

Shaw v. Hunt, U.S. Dist. Lexis 11102 (1994).

Shaw v. Reno, 509 U.S. 630 (1993).

South Carolina v. Katzenbach, 383 U.S. 301 (1966).

Thornburg v. Gingles, 478 U.S. 30 (1986).

United Jewish Organizations v. Carey, 430 U.S. 144 (1977).

United States v. Hays, 115 S. Ct. 2431 (1995).

Vera v. Richards, U.S. Dist. Lexis 12334 (1994).

White v. Regester, 412 U.S. 755 (1973).

Zimmer v. McKeithen, 485 F.2d 1297 (5th Cir. 1973).

INDEX

Addabbo, Joe, 31, 103–4
AFL-CIO. *See* Committee on Political
   Education (COPE)
African Americans: partisanship of, 59, 76–
   78. *See also* black representatives;
   majority-minority districts
Aid to Families with Dependent Children
   (AFDC), 78
Alabama, 4, 131; first black representative of,
   12, 99; 1990s redistricting in, 104–6, 111–
   12; nineteenth-century gerrymanders of,
   19–20
Allen v. State Board of Elections, 9, 30
American Conservative Union (ACU),
   68
Americans for Democratic Action (ADA),
   68, 79
Anaya, Tony, 41
Arizona, 102
Arkansas: nineteenth-century gerrymanders
   of, 21
attorney general, 5–6

Badillo, Herman, 22, 49, 65
backlash. *See* white backlash
Beer v. United States, 28, 30, 126, 130
Bentley, Helen Delich, 112
Berman, Howard, 32
Birmingham, 104
Bishop, Sanford, 129
black influence districts. *See* influence
   districts
black majority districts. *See* majority-minority
   districts
black representatives: alliances with white
   Democrats by, 101–2; election of, 41–48;
   ideology of, 69–70; majority-minority
   districts and, 23, 41–48; margins of victory
   of, 58; 1990s redistricting and increase
   in, 109–10; in 1996, 26; nonracial variables
   and, 43–45; number of, 22, 109, 120;
   party of, 58; percent in House and, 25,
   27–28; percent black and, 41–48; percent
   Latino and, 45, 47, 121; pre-1950, 18;
   primary defeats of, 64, 139n.14; probability
   of election of, 46–47; retirements of, 64–
   65; substantive representation and, 97;

seniority of, 63–65; in white majority
   districts, 41–42
Bond, Julian, 100
Bonilla, Henry, 32, 61, 66
Boggs, Lindy, 31, 33, 103
born-again Christians, 93, 122
Bositis, David, 112
Brooke, Edward, 58, 136n.3
Bullock, Charles, 88, 113, 141n.15
Bush, George, 77, 138n.11
Bush v. Vera, 12, 119, 127–8
Bustamante, Albert, 32, 61

California, 126; Thirty-Third District of, 50;
   Twentieth District of, 32; Twenty-Sixth
   District of, 32
candidate style, 100
Carmines, Edward G., 59
Carnes, John, 42
Carter, Jimmy, 77
Catholics, 93, 122
Chamber of Commerce (CCUS), 68
Chaves, Dennis, 21
Chicago, 18, 53, 135n.3
citizenship, 49
Civil Rights Act of 1964, 59, 92
Clark, Robert, 31
Clay, William, 64
Clayton, Eva, 106–8
Clinton, Bill, 10, 70, 77
Coleman, Ronald, 32, 48–49
Committee on Political Education (COPE),
   68, 79
compactness, 102, 126
"compelling governmental interest," 124–25,
   127
computers, 102
Congress, 6; responsiveness to blacks of, 72
Congressional Black Caucus, 70, 101, 123–24
conservatives, 8
Conyers, John, 64
court cases, 124–33
covered jurisdictions, 4
Crane, Phil, 79
Cuban-American representatives: ideology
   of, 70–71, 143n.28; number of, 22; party of,
   61; seniority of, 66